ALCOHOLICS ANONYMOUS

CULT
OR
CURE?

by
Charles Bufe

With an Introduction by
Dr. Albert Ellis

See Sharp Press ★ San Francisco ★ 1991

For further information contact: See Sharp Press, P.O. Box 6118,
San Francisco, CA 94101.

FIRST PRINTING

Bufe, Charles.
    Alcoholics Anonymous: cult or cure? / Charles Bufe; with an introduction by Dr.
Albert Ellis. — San Francisco: See Sharp, 1991.

    Includes bibliographical references (p. 146-153) and index.
    1. Alcoholics Anonymous. 2. Alcoholics — Rehabilitation. 3. Cults — Psychological
Aspects. 4. Alcoholism — Religious aspects. 5. Alcoholism — Psychological aspects.
6. Alcoholism — Treatment. 7. Oxford Group. 8. Psychology, Religious. 9. Moral
Re-Armament. I. Title. II. Ellis, Albert. Case against religiosity. III. The Case
against religiosity. IV. Alcoholics Anonymous, cult or cure?

                            362.29286

ISBN 0-9613289-3-2
OCLC #23436803

    We would like to thank the following for permission to reprint their copy-
righted materials:

Dr. Albert Ellis and the Institute for Rational Emotive Therapy for permission to
reprint *The Case Against Religiosity*. Copyright 1983, Institute for Rational Emotive
Therapy.

Jack Trimpey and Rational Recovery for permission to reprint "Central Ideas of
Alcoholism." Copyright 1990 Rational Recovery.

Jim Christopher and Secular Organizations for Sobriety for permission to reprint
"Suggested Guidelines for Sobriety." Copyright 1990 Secular Organizations for Sobriety.

Jean Kirkpatrick and Women for Sobriety for permission to reprint "13 Statements
of Acceptance." Copyright 1976, 1987 Jean Kirkpatrick.

"A Humanist Alternative to A.A.'s Twelve Steps," by B.F. Skinner first appeared in
the July/August 1987 issue of *The Humanist* and is reprinted by permission.

The material reprinted on page 25 from "A God-Guided Dictator." Copyright 1936
Christian Century Foundation. Reprinted by permission from the September 9, 1936
issue of *The Christian Century*.

The excerpt reprinted on page 83 from *Prison or Paradise? The New Religious Cults*, copyright © A. James Rudin and Marcia R. Rudin, by permission of Augsburg Fortress.

Design and pre-press production by Typesetting Etc., San Francisco. Printed by
Thomson-Shore, Inc., Dexter, Michigan.

Printed on recycled, acid-free paper with soy-based ink.

Contents

Introduction (by Dr. Albert Ellis) 5

Foreword 9

1. A Typical A.A. Meeting 13

2. The Oxford Group Movement: The Forerunner of A.A. 16

3. A Brief History of A.A. 34

4. The Oxford Groups & A.A.: Similarities & Differences 55

5. The 12 Steps 62

6. The 12 Traditions 73

7. Is A.A. a Cult? (preliminary considerations) 82

8. Is A.A. a Cult? (conclusions) 92

9. How Effective is A.A.? 103

10. The Future of A.A. 115

APPENDIXES

A. Secular Alternatives to A.A. 123

B. Secular Alternatives to the 12 Steps 128

C. The Case Against Religiosity (by Dr. Albert Ellis) 134

Bibliography 146

Index 154

Introduction

Books on Alcoholics Anonymous are usually quite biased—written by either A.A.'s fervent supporters or its ardent detractors. Of all that I have read, the present one by Charles Bufe is the most objective, sensible, and readable. The author has his own political biases, but he holds them well in check and doesn't let them seriously interfere with his evaluations of the theory and practice of A.A.

Charles Bufe's analysis of the history, growth, and future of A.A. is brief but comprehensive. Readers are likely to be exceptionally well-informed, as well as often fascinated, by his incisive treatment of the religious origins of A.A., of its cultish aspects, of its effectiveness and non-effectiveness, and of its likely future. They will also be enlightened by his sensible analyses of A.A.'s 12-Step program and its 12 Traditions.

My own involvement with treating alcoholics goes back many years; and, frankly, was notably unsuccessful from 1943 to 1953, when I was mainly psychoanalytic in my treatment methods. Consequently, I showed addicts that they were traumatized by their early childhood experiences, especially by bad experiences with their alcoholic mothers and fathers, and that if they got insight into these early traumas they would be able to stop their addiction. This form of treatment—now, alas, still largely adopted by Alanon and by Adult Children of Alcoholics—helped my alcoholic clients very little; so I gave it up and in 1955 originated and started practicing rational-emotive therapy (RET), and soon achieved much better results with addicts and with other disturbed individuals.

Like many other psychologists, I have seen a large number of A.A. members over the years, and have found that some of them were distinctly benefitted by A.A. attendance and by their following A.A.'s 12-Step program. Unfortunately, I also found that a high percentage of them developed a special kind of A.A.-type neurosis, including bigoted and devout devotion to the disease concept of alcoholism, to dependency on imagined Higher Powers instead of on themselves, to damning their parents for "making" them alcoholics, to defining themselves and almost everyone else in the world as codependents and as some kind of addict, and to other kinds of disturbances. I also found that many of my quite intelligent and irreligious alcoholic clients were rather nauseated by the fanatical religiosity of A.A. and therefore soon quit going to its meetings and were forced to do without any kind of support group. Similarly, many of my clients who were in other 12-Step programs — especially those in Overeaters Anonymous — were either turned off to the religiosity of these programs or became seriously addicted to and overly dependent on such programs.

In 1985, when I was asked to review the seventeenth printing of the Third Edition of *Alcoholics Anonymous* (the "Big Book"), I wrote a review for the *Employee Assistance Quarterly* (1985, 1, 95-97) entitled, "Why Alcoholics Anonymous is Probably Doing Itself and Alcoholics More Harm Than Good by Its Insistence on a Higher Power." In this review, I briefly criticized the Higher Power aspects of the 12 Steps and found them often to be distinctly iatrogenic [that is, a form of treatment which in itself causes problems to those being treated].

In the same year, Dr. Eugene Schoenfeld, a psychiatrist who had been working in the field of alcohol addiction for a number of years, suggested that we collaborate on a paper, "Divine Intervention and the Treatment of Chemical Dependency." We finished the paper quickly but for the next several years could not find a professional journal, among the leading publications we submitted it to, courageous enough to print it. Virtually all of them, expecially those in the field of addiction, thought that the paper was fine but were afraid of great objections by A.A. partisans if they dared to publish it. Finally, the *Journal of Substance Abuse* agreed to accept it, providing that Gene and I would also let them publish, in the same issue, no less than five replies by A.A. supporters. We thought that this was a bit much, but having no other choice, we agreed and our article was finally published (*Journal of Substance Abuse*, 1990, 2, 459-468, 489-494).

Meanwhile, in 1986 I and my associates at the Institute for Rational-Emotive Therapy in New York started to write a textbook, *Rational-Emotive Treatment of Alcoholic and Drug Abusers* (New York: Pergamon, 1988), that presented the RET approach to these forms of addiction. But we were warned by the publisher not to knock A.A., because that would jeopardize the distribution and sale of the book. So we blue-penciled our objections to some of the 12-Step programs.

1985 seems to have been a banner year for RET and alcoholism treatment because in that year Jack Trimpey, a practitioner of RET for many years, and a licensed clinical social worker in California, worked on himself to become a recovered alcoholic and started Rational

Recovery (R.R.), a self-help organization which includes some of the best features of A.A. but completely omits any allegiance to God, to a Higher Power, or to any other kind of addictive dependency, including dependency on R.R. itself. Like Women for Sobriety, Men for Sobriety, and Secular Organizations for Sobriety (S.O.S.), Rational Recovery offers a real alternative to people seeking a self-help, anti-addiction group that is entirely free from religious dogma and dependency. In addition, it tries to arrange that each of its many self-help groups has an RET consultant and that all the group members learn some of the basic principles and practices of rational-emotive therapy, so that they can stay off addictive substances and also can work to overcome their cognitive-emotive-behavioral disturbances that very frequently drive them to become and to stay alcoholic. So although I favor all nonreligious alternatives to A.A., I naturally especially favor Rational Recovery. [For information on these nonreligious alternatives to A.A., see appendixes A & B.]

Back to Charles Bufe. Although it is hardly an encyclopedia on A.A.'s history and functioning, his book succinctly and very adequately gives a sound picture of its workings. It can usefully be read by virtually every addict and by anyone else who wants a fine understanding of the advantages and limitations of the 12-Step programs. I am delighted to have been in contact with the author while he was working on this book, and I believe that he has turned out a valuable addition to the alcoholism literature.

—Albert Ellis, Ph.D., President
Institute for Rational-Emotive Therapy
45 East 65th Street
New York, NY 10021

Foreword

Alcoholics Anonymous is the most influential self-help organization for alcoholics in the United States. It is commonly believed to be the most effective treatment for alcoholism; many believe that it is the *only* effective treatment for alcoholism. It is also the basis for a great many inpatient and outpatient alcoholism treatment programs, and is an important, often mandatory, adjunct to many others; and a very high proportion of the alcoholism professionals staffing those programs are former alcoholics who recovered via A.A. As well, the media almost universally accord A.A. respectful, indeed reverential, treatment.

Still, remarkably little useful information about Alcoholics Anonymous is available to the public, and what little there is comes from A.A. itself and from its numerous allies. While A.A. and its supporters, with rare exceptions, do not deliberately disseminate false information, they do, naturally enough, disseminate only those facts and opinions which reflect favorably upon A.A. This has resulted in many false impressions becoming part of "the conventional wisdom."

One such impression is the belief that A.A.'s co-founder, Bill Wilson, invented A.A.'s 12-Step program from whole cloth. Nothing could be further from the truth. Another false impression is the idea that from its inception A.A. developed as an independent organization, when in fact it developed within another organization, the Oxford Group Movement/Moral Re-Armament, and operated as part of the Oxford Group Movement for the first few years of its existence.

This fact is fleetingly, if at all, mentioned in most histories of Alcoholics Anonymous, and when it is acknowledged, the information provided about the Oxford Groups is usually so incomplete as to be misleading. When the Oxford Group Movement is mentioned, more often than not it's simply referred to as an "evangelical Christian group," or something similar. While this description is accurate as far as it goes, it's in the same league with a description of Adolf Hitler as "a controversial politician who led Germany from 1933 to 1945."

While these descriptions of Hitler and the Oxford Groups contain no outright lies, much more information is necessary to provide true pictures of both the "evangelical Christian group" and the "politician." So, in light of the Oxford Groups' importance in the history of Alcoholics Anonymous, one major focus of this book will be upon the Oxford Group Movement and its relationship to A.A.

Another focus of this book will be upon A.A.'s efficacy as a method of alcoholism treatment. A.A. is routinely presented in the media as the most effective treatment for alcoholism, and one that is applicable to all alcohol abusers. Is this in fact the case? A major purpose of this book is to sort through the studies and other evidence of A.A.'s effectiveness in order to determine the facts; and again, the facts which emerge paint a picture far different from that routinely presented in the mass media.

A.A.'s critics, too, have at times painted inaccurate images of the organization, portraying it as a "cult." In order to answer this accusation, two of this book's chapters are devoted to analyzing the characteristics of cults such as Synanon, Scientology, and the People's Temple, and to comparing them with the characteristics of Alcoholics Anonymous. The portrait of A.A. which emerges from this comparison provides a truer and more revealing image of the organization than those painted by either its friends or by some of its critics.

A final purpose of this book is to analyze A.A.'s program and structure with a view to distinguishing its strengths and weaknesses. It's paradoxical, but A.A. has drawn much undeserved applause over the years for vastly overrated accomplishments, while at the same time its very real strengths have gone largely unrecognized and unappreciated. This is truly unfortunate in that many of A.A.'s useful features, particularly its organizational principles and organizational structure, could be fruitfully adopted in a far wider social and political sphere than that of alcoholism self-help groups. The irony of the situation is that these healthy A.A. principles and structures are all but ignored, while the A.A. principles contained in the 12 Steps are being loudly trumpeted as a panacea for the world's ills.

Clearly there is much to be learned from A.A., and what I've attempted in this study is to note the most obvious lessons. My hope is that both A.A.'s friends and foes will accept this book for what it is, an honest evaluation by an investigator with decidedly mixed feelings about A.A. In particular, I hope that A.A.'s friends will not reject this evaluation out of hand because, as A.A.'s co-founders might have put it, a little deflation every now and then can be a good thing.

Finally, I would like to thank all of those who helped to make this book possible. I would particularly like to thank the staff of the Alcoholics Anonymous General Service Office, who have been helpful and open in answering my questions; Dr. Albert Ellis, who provided many useful criticisms as this book was being written and who has also been good enough to write the introduction and to grant permission to reprint his essay, "The Case Against Religiosity," as an appendix; Lynaea Search, for a fine copy editing job; Jim Christopher, for his interest and helpful comments; J.R. Swanson and Chris Carlsson, for help with the cover design; the reference staff of the San Francisco Public Library, who processed dozens of interlibrary loan requests for me; Earl Lee, for useful suggestions on cult literature and for help with cataloguing the book; Greg Williamson, for help with proofreading; and Kata Orndorff, for help with proofreading and the many useful suggestions and criticisms she made while I was researching and writing this book.

— Charles Bufe

1

A Typical A.A. Meeting

What is a "typical" A.A. meeting like? Is there such a thing? A look in the A.A. "meeting book" for any large metropolitan area reveals a bewildering variety of meetings. A recent San Francisco meeting book, for example, lists meetings seven days a week with the first starting at 6 a.m. and the last starting at midnight; it lists beginners' meetings, step meetings, open meetings, closed meetings, speaker meetings, discussion meetings, candlelight meetings, women's meetings, lesbian and gay meetings, nonsmokers' meetings, writers' and artists' meetings, meetings for retired seamen, meetings conducted in Spanish—there are even meetings for atheists and agnostics.[1]

Meeting places range from church basements, to library conference rooms, to hotel lobbies, to rented halls. Meeting sizes range from as few as three or four people up to several hundred at the larger weekend meetings. About all that can be said with reasonable certainty is that meetings last an hour to an hour and a half, and even that's not always the case. Still, certain features are common to virtually all A.A. meetings, and there are many other features which, while not universal, are typical.

If you were to go to a meeting you selected at random, it would probably go something like this:

It's ten minutes before meeting time as you walk through the front door of the A.A. hall, a large, dingy room reeking of stale tobacco smoke. You walk across the grimy linoleum floor to the coffee urn, pour yourself a cup of what appears to be used motor oil (rumor has it that the stuff will dissolve pencils), grab a couple of cookies, and wander over to one of the forty or so folding metal chairs facing the table at the front of the room.

The meeting's secretary and the evening's speaker are already seated at the table, smoking cigarettes and slurping coffee. Other people, mostly casually dressed men in their 30s and 40s, are filing in, gradually filling the seats, and gradually filling the air with tobacco smoke. Perhaps half the chairs are taken when the meeting starts.

Precisely on the hour the secretary raps his gavel, introduces himself, and asks two pre-selected members to read the A.A. Preamble and the Serenity Prayer. Then, since it's a small meeting, everyone in the room introduces himself or herself and is then greeted by the crowd: "My name is Mike. I'm an alcoholic." "Hi Mike!" "My name is Bob. Alcoholic." "Hi Bob!" "Ed, alcoholic." "Hi Ed!". . . until everyone present has stated his or her name and muttered the magic word, "alcoholic." The secretary then asks any newcomers with less than 30 days sobriety to introduce themselves; he adds that this is only so that the rest of the members can get to know them. One hand timidly goes up in the back row and, after being prompted by the secretary, its owner introduces himself as "Tom"; everyone else loudly echoes, "Hi Tom," and applauds. The secretary next asks if there are any out-of-towners at the meeting. Since there are none, he goes on to ask if anyone has an anniversary (of months or years of sobriety) that day. No one does, so the secretary concludes by making his only announcement, that of an upcoming "clean and sober" dance at a local A.A. hangout.

The speaker rises, steps to the podium, introduces himself, and launches into a history of his alcoholism, describing at length and with apparent relish some of his more lurid drinking episodes. He pauses, lights a cigarette, and speaks of how he "bottomed out"—the degradation, humiliation, and hopelessness he felt when he finally realized what alcohol had done to him. He lights another cigarette and recounts how finally, in desperation, he hesitantly walked into an A.A. meeting despite fears about "the God stuff." Deeply inhaling a hit of tobacco smoke, he describes how his life has never been the same since that day. He kept coming to meetings, even though he still had doubts, because he was attracted to "something" the A.A. members had which he felt lacking in himself. He lights another cigarette and continues, saying that once he overcame his doubts, began to work the Steps, and found his "Higher Power," his life has been transformed. He sits down to polite applause as his cigarette smoke curls upward toward the humming fluorescent lights.

By this time there are only 25 minutes left, and the secretary throws the meeting open to questions and discussion. A hand goes up in the front row and a nearly incoherent but boastful drunkalogue (a recitation of drunken escapades) ensues for ten minutes. Toward the end of it, the secretary passes the collection basket; most of those present chip in a buck or some pocket change. The next member to speak, who has been chafing at the bit during the drunkalogue, takes off on a tangent and describes how by working one of the Steps he overcame his frustration after a car accident. One or two others take off on different tangents, and then it's time to end the meeting.

The secretary announces the fact and everyone rises, joins hands, and most say the Lord's Prayer. About a quarter, looking pained or disgusted, remain mute. After a moment of silence everyone chants, "Keep coming back. It works!" And the meeting is over.

About half of those present leave immediately, while a few busy themselves cleaning up the room, and the rest stand around drinking coffee, smoking cigarettes, and chatting, two of them paying special attention to the newcomer. Finally, a half-hour after the meeting formally closed, the secretary ushers everyone out into the night.

Not all meetings are like this, however—just a majority. Other writers have described supportive meetings with friendly socializing in a cozy, club-like atmosphere.[2] Such meetings exist in abundance, but in my estimation they're outnumbered by meetings of the type I've described here.

I should also point out that only those who blindly, and vocally, embrace the 12 Steps are fully welcome at most meetings. Those who have doubts and those who have disagreements with A.A. dogma are normally ostracized if they express their opinions; and those who remain silent and sit on their doubts will normally be the objects of proselytization and, if they continue to refuse to mouth accepted A.A. wisdom, will win, at best, grudging acceptance—if they're strong enough to stand up to the ridicule and condescension they're sure to encounter.

If doubters are fortunate, there will be an "agnostics" or "atheists" meeting in their city where they can commune with their fellow second-class citizens; but such meetings are normally found only in large cities such as San Francisco. In many, probably most, rural areas, small towns, and small cities, a majority of meetings are even more overtly religious than the one I've described here.

---

1. "Step meetings" feature discussion of the 12 Steps; at "open meetings" both alcoholics and nonalcoholics are welcome; and at "closed meetings" only alcoholics are welcome. The names of the other types of meetings are self-explanatory.
2. See, for example, *Getting Better*, by Nan Robertson. New York: William Morrow and Company, 1988. Chapter 5, pp. 109-126.

2

The Oxford Group
Movement:
The Forerunner of A.A.

"...many a channel had been used by Providence to create Alcoholics Anonymous. And none had been more vitally needed than the one opened through Sam Shoemaker and his Oxford Group associates ...the early A.A. got its ideas of self-examination, acknowledgement of character defects, restitution for harm done, and working with others straight from the Oxford Groups and directly from Sam Shoemaker, their former leader in America, and from nowhere else ...A.A. owes a debt of timeless gratitude for all that God sent us through Sam and his friends in the days of A.A.'s infancy."

— Bill Wilson in *Alcoholics Anonymous Comes of Age*, pp. 39-40

In order to understand Alcoholics Anonymous, it's first necessary to understand the movement which gave birth to A.A.: the Oxford Group Movement, also known as the Oxford Groups, Buchmanism, and, in its later days, Moral Re-Armament (MRA). The importance of the Oxford Group Movement to the structure, practices, and, especially, the ideology of Alcoholics Anonymous cannot be overstated. The two founders of A.A., Bill Wilson and Dr. Robert Smith were enthusiastic members of the Oxford Groups; the early A.A.-to-be groups in both Akron and New York operated within the Oxford Groups; and both Bill Wilson and "Dr. Bob" believed that the principles of the Oxford Groups were the key to overcoming alcoholism. Thus, A.A.'s bible, *Alcoholics Anonymous*, the so-called Big Book, in large part reads like a piece of Oxford Group Movement literature, and the 12 Steps, the cornerstone of A.A. ideology, are for all intents and purposes a codification of Oxford Group principles.

The Oxford Group Movement was very much the creature of its founder, Dr. Frank Nathan Daniel Buchman. He was born on June 4, 1878 in Pennsburg, Pennsylvania, of conservative, apparently prosperous, Lutheran parents. He attended Muhlenberg College in

Allentown, Pennsylvania and graduated in 1899. Following his studies at Muhlenberg, he entered Mount Airy Seminary (Pennsylvania) and graduated in 1902 as an ordained Lutheran minister.

Buchman's first parish was in Overbrook, a suburb of Philadelphia, where shortly after his appointment he opened a small hospice for young men. The hospice apparently prospered, because in June 1905 the Evangelical Lutheran Ministerium of Pennsylvania and Adjacent States called upon him to open a larger hospice for young men in Philadelphia. He proceeded to do so, but the enterprise was plagued by financial problems. In 1908 he became embroiled in a dispute with the Ministerium's Finance Committee and resigned his position in a huff.

Shortly after resigning, he went to an evangelical conference in Keswick, England (probably at his parents' expense). While there he had a "conversion experience" complete with "a poignant vision of the Crucified" while listening to a Salvation Army speaker at a local chapel. Following this experience, he wrote letters of apology to the six members of the Ministerium with whom he had quarreled. (In Oxford Group/Moral Re-Armament literature, much is made of the fact that he received not a single reply. But according to the superintendent of the Ministerium, Dr. J.F. Ohl, world-traveler Buchman didn't bother to put a return address on his letters.[1]) He also "shared" his experience with the family with which he was staying, thus making his first convert, their son.

After returning from England, he applied for and was given a position as YMCA secretary at State College, Pennsylvania as of July 1, 1909. At that time the "Y" was more than a series of health clubs; it was an active evangelical association with considerable influence on American college campuses. Buchman built a reputation at State College for conducting well-attended Bible classes and evangelical crusades, and for building up the membership of the YMCA. According to one report, he inflated "Y" membership figures by handing out "free" Bibles to incoming freshmen and by later billing them for "Y" dues.[2] He also instituted the practice of the "Morning Watch" (later called "Quiet Time") in which devotees spent time reading the Bible, praying, and "listening to God."

In 1915 he resigned to go traveling once again, this time to the Far East with evangelist Sherwood Eddy. Upon his return in 1916, he was appointed Extension Lecturer in Personal Evangelism at the Hartford (Connecticut) Seminary. At first, he lived in the students' dormitory—a rather odd thing for a man of 38 to do—but he was asked to move out after students complained of his intrusive meth-

ods. He also began to rely on "guidance" (from God) to run his daily
life, and encouraged students to do the same. In this way he developed a reputation for being unreliable — "God" would "guide" him
to miss appointments, etc., etc. — and students were supposedly
"guided" to do things such as booking steamship passage to Europe
without having the funds to pay for it.[3] One former Buchmanite
later recalled, "I put my trust in guidance and failed my examina-
tions."[4] Buchman also gained a reputation for dwelling on the
importance of sexual sin in his dealings with students.

To make matters worse, he was having trouble with members of
the faculty at Hartford. Buchman was an evangelical fundamentalist
who emphasized emotional experience, and he regarded the classes of
his colleagues as not "vital." They returned the contempt by
regarding Buchman as a simpleton.

So, it seems probable that this was not an especially happy period
in Buchman's life; and he must have been at least somewhat relieved
when he received the "guidance" to resign his position. In 1922 he
quit his job at Hartford in order to devote himself to "personal
evangelism" and to living off the largesse of wealthy backers, activities which he would pursue for the rest of his life. Buchman remained
unrepentant about his lavish lifestyle, and that of his close associates,
to the end of his days. On many occasions he made remarks similar
to one quoted in *Time* in 1936: "Why shouldn't we stay in 'posh'
hotels? Isn't God a millionaire?"[5]

While at Hartford, Buchman had much free time, and thus
opportunity to travel. In Kuling, China in 1918, he organized his
first "houseparty," a type of gathering which was to become a
Buchmanite trademark. Houseparties were in some ways a form of
religious retreat and were, at least for their first decade or so, gather-
ings of no more than a few dozen people in spacious private homes
or, more often, expensive inns or hotels. Participants were normally
invited to attend through friends or acquaintances already involved
with Buchman's movement.

The atmosphere at houseparties was always informal, and activities ranged from Bible study and "quiet times" to bridge playing
and golf. There were also voluntary general meetings in which
attendees "shared," confessing their "sins" and offering witness to the
"change" in their lives caused by adherence to Buchman's principles.
A noteworthy feature of houseparties was the upscale economic
status of their attendees, and the frequent well-advertised presence of
prominent individuals. It was the norm for Buchman and his cohorts
to go to great lengths to attract the rich and famous, and, when they

were hooked, to shamelessly exploit their names, a tendency which would become more pronounced in the coming years.

While still at Hartford Seminary, Buchman began to hold house-parties at Ivy League colleges in the U.S. and at Oxford and Cambridge in England. This was entirely in keeping with Buchman's background as a YMCA secretary at State College and as a lecturer at Hartford Seminary. Through the mid-1920s, the focus of his ministry would be evangelical work at colleges such as Harvard, Yale, Princeton and Bryn Mawr. Throughout this period, Buchman retained his obsession with sex. One Harvard graduate is reported to have said, "He started asking me intimate questions about sex before I'd been alone with him for five minutes. I left in a hurry."[6]

In 1924, Buchman's sexual obsession and the obtrusive zeal of some of his converts caused Princeton University's president to ban him. As was usual in his campus crusades, Buchman's followers engaged in high-pressure attempts to get fellow students to "change," followed dubious "guidance" religiously, with predictable social and academic results, thought nothing of invading other students' privacy, and engaged in inappropriate "sharing," much of it of a sexual nature. One chronicler reports that a Buchmanite took "the young and rather innocent daughter" of a Princeton professor out on a date, and proceeded to "share" with her a confession of his sexual sins in fulsome detail.[7]

Such incidents did little to increase Frank Buchman's popularity with either students or faculty. Buchman himself, though, seems to have precipitated his own banishment by telling John Hibden, Princeton's president, that 85 percent of Princeton undergraduates were either "sexually perverted or [self-]abusive."[8] Hibden evidently didn't appreciate this assessment of his students, and soon declared Buchman persona non grata at Princeton.[9] While this undoubtedly annoyed Buchman, it certainly didn't deter him from pursuing his "good work" at other colleges. But by the mid-'20s, the influence of the Buchman movement had peaked on American campuses, and it quickly faded into obscurity at virtually every institution where it had taken root.

Throughout what could be termed the "collegiate" period of the Oxford Group Movement, Buchman's program was remarkably consistent. It consisted of "personal evangelism" with emphases upon: 1) both public and private confession of sin, with an emphasis upon sexual sin; 2) reception of divine "guidance" during "quiet times"; 3) complete surrender to this "guidance"; 4) the living of a "guided" life in which every aspect of one's actions, down to the choice of dinner entree, was controlled by God; 5) practice of the Buchmanite "four absolutes"—purity, honesty, love, and unselfishness; 6) making restitution to those one has harmed; and 7) carrying "the message" to those still "defeated."

The "message" was delivered one-to-one by individual Buchmanite "life changers," also known as "soul surgeons," or en masse by "traveling teams" which ranged in size from about half-a-dozen to several dozen persons. These teams would spread the word on campuses through individual contacts and through the ever-popular houseparties. A notable feature of the Buchmanite movement at this stage was that it was directed at the "up-and-out" on prestigious campuses, and that on those campuses its primary aim was to convert "key men"—football stars and other athletes, student body officers, and the sons of the prominent, the powerful, and the very rich.

During this period four other key features of Buchmanism became prominent: its emphasis on nonprofessionalism; its antipathy toward formal organization; its complete failure to consider political, social and economic causes of individual and social problems; and its virulent anti-intellectualism. The emphasis on nonprofessionalism was implicit in the concept of divine "guidance" available to all who would listen, and the accompanying command that all "guided" individuals should "change" others. The antipathy to formal organization was also implicit in the concept of "guidance." (If individuals are being directly controlled by God, what need do they have for formal organization?) What this led to in practice was dictatorial control of the movement by Buchman and a small clique surrounding him. The neglect of political, social, and economic factors as causes of individual and social problems was due to Buchman's belief that "guidance" in itself was sufficient to solve all problems, and to his belief in social inequality—that there is nothing inherently wrong with coercion, domination and submission, with some giving orders and others taking them, and with an unequal distribution of wealth and income. And the anti-intellectualism of his message likewise stemmed from his fixation on "guidance" as a cureall. Anything which could call "guidance" into doubt was inherently undesirable; thus logic, careful consideration of facts, and a questioning attitude were deadly enemies to the Oxford Group Movement. A Group axiom expresses this attitude succinctly: "Doubt stifles and makes abortive our attempt to act upon God's Guidance."[10] A former Buchmanite recalled that when he was a member of the Groups, "thinking seemed to me atheism."[11]

Following the collapse of his campus movement in the U.S.,

Buchman moved his base of operations to England and conducted evangelical crusades at Oxford and Cambridge. It was through recruits garnered in these crusades that the group acquired its name. While the Buchman movement never attracted more than a small minority of students at Oxford, a traveling team consisting largely of Oxford students went to South Africa in 1929 where it was dubbed "the Oxford Group" by the press; and shortly after that Buchman and his minions began to refer to themselves as the "Oxford Group Movement." Whether this was "absolutely honest" is open to question: Buchman had never studied at Oxford University; he held no position there; and his movement had no official connection with the university and very limited influence among its students.

Nonetheless, the use of the Oxford name was very advantageous to the Buchmanites, suggesting as it did connection with a venerable and respected institution. Another advantage was that the centenary of the Oxford Movement—John Henry Newman's attempt to Catholicize the Anglican Church—was to be celebrated in 1933, and the names Oxford Movement and Oxford Group Movement would inevitably become confused in the public mind, much to the benefit of the Oxford Group Movement. The Buchmanites used the name Oxford Group Movement for ten years, and dropped it only in the opening days of World War II for all but certain legal purposes.

Concurrent with the transfer of his base of operations to England, Buchman began to shift the focus of his movement on both sides of the Atlantic from well-to-do students to their parents. In the early 1930s, the Buchman movement began to hold mass meetings which, like the much smaller meetings of the 1920s, were called "houseparties." For several years the Buchmanites held an annual houseparty in Oxford. Attendance in 1930 was 700; by 1935 it had risen to 10,000. In 1936 a houseparty in Birmingham, England attracted 15,000 persons. The smaller '20s-style houseparties were, however, also a prominent feature of the Oxford Group Movement throughout the 1930s.

A feature common to both types was the ostentatious use of the names of the rich and famous. One friendly observer noted, "No feature of the Oxford Group Movement so strikes the casual observer...as its studious attention to position, title, and social prestige. No meeting is properly launched without its quota of patrons of rank and social standing."[12] In the U.S., prominent—and trumpeted—supporters included Russell Firestone, Mr. and Mrs. Henry Ford, Mrs. Thomas Edison, Admiral Byrd, Mr. and Mrs. Cleveland Dodge, and Mrs. Harry Guggenheim.

Another notable feature of the Oxford Group Movement in this period (and indeed throughout its history) was its routine and extreme exaggeration of its own importance and influence. The Groupists' estimation of their influence in South Africa is illustrative. During the years following 1929, when Buchman accompanied the "team" (and the Buchman movement acquired the name "Oxford Group" there), "traveling teams" visited South Africa many times. In his estimate of the Buchmanites' influence, Deputy Prime Minister J.H. Hofmeyr, who had fallen under Buchman's sway, stated that Buchman's 1929 visit had "started a major and continuing influence for racial reconciliation throughout the whole country, white and black, Dutch and British."[13] Similar estimations were made after every "traveling team" visit.

The South Africans, curiously, didn't seem to notice the effect of the Buchmanites. Writing in the South African religious newspaper, *The Church Times*, on September 14, 1934, the Cape Town correspondent stated: "The English newspapers continually bring us news of the wonders which the Group Movement is effecting in South Africa. To it they ascribe the formation of the coalition Government, and the melting away of the barriers between Dutch and English, European and native, Indian and Bantu;...It is curious that in South Africa we should know so little of these wonders. It seems clear to us that the coalition Government came into being through sheer weariness of strife; certainly it was never attributed here to the influence of the Groups. And the Groups have long since ceased to attract any attention to speak of."[14]

Undeterred by facts, Oxford Group Movement/Moral Re-Armament (MRA) spokesmen continued to give glowing accounts of their effectiveness in healing racial divisions in South Africa over the coming years. In 1955, South African delegates attended a Moral Re-Armament World Assembly in Washington, D.C. The Allentown *Morning Call*, Buchman's hometown newspaper, reported: "Speakers from South Africa said MRA was replacing racial supremacy and bloody revolution with 'a new dimension of racial unity.'"[15] As late as 1960 Frank Buchman wrote in his birthday message, "A Hurricane of Common Sense," that, "White and black leadership in South Africa want their Cabinet and the whole country to see this movie [the MRA film, *The Crowning Experience*]. They say it holds the secret that alone can cure the racial divisions that are tearing South Africa apart, dividing her from other countries, and undermining her economic life."[16] This was written when the *apartheid* system had already been in place for over a decade, and less than a year before the Sharpeville massacre. Yet Buchman makes no demand that the *apartheid* system be dismantled; in fact, he makes no criticism of it at all. In his view it was enough that the South Africans see his MRA film.

Such political naïvete was nothing new to Buchman. In 1936, at the height of his movement's prestige and influence, he stated in an interview published in the August 26, 1936 *New York World Telegram*:

> "I thank heaven for a man like Adolf Hitler, who built a front line of defence against the anti-Christ of Communism...
>
> "Of course I don't condone everything the Nazis do. Anti-semitism? Bad, naturally. I suppose Hitler sees a Karl Marx in every Jew.
>
> "But think what it would mean to the world if Hitler surrendered to the control of God. Or Mussolini. Or any dictator. Through such a man God could control a nation overnight and solve every last, bewildering problem...
>
> "...Human problems aren't economic. They're moral and they can't be solved by immoral measures. They could be solved within a God-controlled democracy, or perhaps I should say a theocracy, and they could be solved through a God-controlled Fascist dictatorship."[17]

It's worth noting that Bill Wilson and his fellow A.A.s-to-be *must* have known about this interview, which caused a public furor, yet they continued to work as part of the Oxford Groups for more than another year in New York, and more than another three years in Akron.

It's also worth noting that A.A., in its official "Conference-approved" biography of Bill Wilson, *Pass It On*, treats this matter in what can only be described as a dishonest manner. This is all the more surprising and disappointing in that the book's dust jacket proclaims, "Every word is documented, every source checked." In the section of *Pass It On* dealing with Buchman's remarks, the anonymous author states:

> "In August [1936], the New York *World Telegram* published an article about Buchman, charging that he was pro-Nazi. The newspaper quoted Buchman as saying: 'Thank heaven for a man like Adolf Hitler who built a front-line defense against the Anti-Christ of Communism. Think what it would mean to the world if Hitler surrendered to God. Through such a man, God could control a nation and solve every problem. Human problems aren't economic, they're moral, and they can't be solved by immoral measures.'
>
> "While most discussions of the incident, even by Buchman's critics, have since vindicated him, the article brought the group into public controversy."[18]

There are several remarkable features in this passage. The first is that the *World Telegram* piece is referred to as an "article," when in fact it was an *interview* in which Buchman's comments comprised well over half the text, with almost all of the remaining text consisting of descriptive passages, transitions between Buchman's statements, and uncontroversial background information on Buchman and the Oxford Group Movement. There is a tremendous difference between an "article" in which Buchman was "charged" with being pro-Nazi, and an *interview* in which he himself clearly expressed pro-Nazi opinions, a fact which undoubtedly was not lost on the author of A.A.'s official Wilson biography.

Another remarkable feature of the passage just quoted from *Pass It On* is that Buchman's statements are carefully edited to put his best possible face forward. The anonymous A.A. author has taken fragments separated by hundreds of words and patched them together as if they were a single statement, while dropping a number of words within the fragments. For example, by dropping the word "But" before the words "think what it would mean . . . ," the author made the fragments appear to fit together snugly — thus hiding the fact that the "statement" is a patchwork.

In normal literary practice, it's considered proper to separate patched-together fragments with ellipses if the intervening material doesn't alter the meaning of the quoted material. If the intervening material does alter the meaning, as it does in the "statement" cited in *Pass It On*, it's considered unethical to quote it even with ellipses, and blatantly dishonest to quote it as if it were a single unitary statement. It should also be noted that the author of *Pass It On* quoted Buchman's "statement" in such a way as to leave the impression that it was the *only* such "statement" in the "article."

Perhaps most remarkably, the anonymous A.A. author concludes that, "most discussions of the incident, even by Buchman's critics, have since vindicated him." One remarkable aspect of this statement is its deliberate fuzziness. What was Buchman "vindicated" of? Of making pro-Nazi statements? Of being pro-Nazi? Our A.A. author leaves that crucial matter unresolved.

Further, I've done my best to read *all* of the widely circulated criticisms of Buchman's remarks, and *none* "vindicate" him of making pro-Nazi statements. I should also point out that Buchman never denied that he made the statements quoted in the *World Telegram*, and that he never repudiated them.[19] (Since he believed that he was "guided" to make the remarks, if he had repudiated them it would have been a tacit admission that the "guidance" he received was in error—which would have brought down his whole ideological house of cards, built as it was on the infallibility of "guidance.")

As for "vindicating" Buchman of being pro-Nazi, several of his critics pointed out that Buchman was a political dunce who believed—as Buchman himself stated in the *World Telegram* interview —that the world's problems could be solved through "a God-controlled democracy," a "theocracy," or a "God-controlled Fascist dictatorship." It must be admitted, though, that in the *World Telegram* interview Buchman showed decided enthusiasm for the latter option.

As *The Christian Century* pointed out two weeks after Buchman's remarks were published:

> "Indeed, perhaps the worst thing about a religion which undertakes to be purely individualistic and to concern itself not at all as to the way in which the corporate life of society is organized is that it cannot succeed in that undertaking—it is forced to take a political position, and its utter lack of understanding of political realities predetermines what that position shall be.
>
> "Such a religion enters the social arena inevitably on the side of reaction. God works through individuals it [Buchmanism] argues. The way to make institutions good is to make the individuals who run them good. The fewer these individuals are, the simpler the operation. The only way to make a good government is to convert the governors, and if there could be but one governor dictating the policies of the nation under God's guidance, the ideal type of state would have been achieved. Individualism in religion thus leads by the straightest road to fascism in politics."[20]

If this is "vindication" of Frank Buchman, it's vindication of a very strange sort.

Another "incident" is also revealing of Buchman's attitude toward the Nazis. At the 1936 Berlin Olympics, Buchman offered to introduce a British MP, Kenneth Lindsay, to Heinrich Himmler, who Buchman referred to as "a great lad."[21] At the time, that "great lad" was the head of the Gestapo. It should be remembered, however, that Buchman always took great pains to ingratiate himself with "key men" of all political persuasions (except Communists). It seems probable that in this incident Buchman was revealing no special love for Himmler, but was simply being his normal, oily self.

Not quite two years after the *World Telegram* interview, Buchman launched his "Moral Rearmament" campaign in Britain on May 28, 1938 in a speech in London. The implication of the slogan "Moral Rearmament" seemed to be that if the people of Britain relied on "guidance," they had no need to physically rearm to fend off Hitler. Three weeks before the Munich conference Buchman coined the slogan "Guns or Guidance" and — remembering that the influence of Buchman's movement was strongest among rich Tories, that is, members of the ruling class — one can only speculate on the possible contribution of Buchman's Moral Rearmament/Guns or Guidance campaign to Chamberlain's policy of appeasement.

Within three years of Buchman's launching the Moral Rearmament campaign, the Buchmanites had abandoned the name Oxford Group Movement for all but certain legal purposes, and the name of Buchman's movement became Moral Re-Armament, or MRA. Coincidentally with the adoption of the MRA name, the Buchmanites shifted their emphasis from "personal evangelism" to mass propaganda through full-page newspaper advertisements, worldwide radio broadcasts, mass distribution of Buchmanite books and pamphlets, and the holding of huge public rallies. This shift in emphasis did little to reverse the declining fortunes of the movement, which had been on a downhill slide since the time of Buchman's "thank heaven for Hitler" remarks in 1936.

A contributory factor to the decline of Buchmanism was the fact that in both the U.S. and Britain during World War II, several dozen Oxford Group members attempted to obtain exemptions from the draft on the grounds that they were "lay evangelists" and that their work was essential to national morale. *None* of these "lay evangelists" were pacifists or conscientious objectors; they actually favored the war, but had been "guided" not to take part in it personally because of the importance of their "work." Their "work" consisted of the production of heavy-handed MRA morality plays with titles such as "You Can Defend America." The authorities were impressed by neither their arguments nor their "chicken hawk" attitude, and the Buchmanite "lay evangelists" were soon wearing khaki and crewcuts and marching in lock-step with other conscripts.[22]

The "Moral Rearmament" campaign, the attempts at draft evasion by MRA members, and Buchman's 1936 interview in which he thanked heaven for Hitler contributed to marked public disenchantment with Buchman and his Groups. A good indication of this decline in interest can be found in the *Reader's Guide to Periodical Literature*. The Jan. 1929-June 1932 volume lists 3 articles on the Oxford Groups; the July 1932-June 1935 volume lists 38 articles on the Groups; the July 1935-June 1937 volume lists 12 pieces on the Oxford Groups; the July 1937-June 1939 volume lists 12 pieces on the Groups; the July 1939-June 1941 volume lists 5 articles on the

Groups; the July 1941-June 1943 volume lists 5 articles on the Groups; and the July 1943-June 1945 volume does not list a single article on either Frank Buchman or the Oxford Groups.

Following the war, Buchman's fortunes revived somewhat and wealthy backers bought luxurious hotels for his movement at Mackinac Island, Michigan and Caux, Switzerland. This isn't surprising. Buchman's doctrine of individual responsibility for all personal and social ills posed absolutely no threat to the wealth of his backers, allowed them to feel virtuous while retaining their privileges, and even showed some prospects of further domesticating the labor movement.

That was a difficult job given the corrupt, hierarchical, and visionless nature of most American and British unions, but the Buchmanites felt themselves up to the task. From the mid-1930s on, one finds numerous Oxford Groups/MRA claims of successful interventions in labor struggles. The scenarios outlined by MRA were quite often drearily the same: One of the parties in a dispute, often a labor "leader," was "changed" by the Buchmanites, realized his wrongs, confessed them to someone on the management side who was so touched by the confession that he confessed his wrongs to the original wrongdoer, and the conflict was peacefully resolved; and wages, working conditions and productivity all improved sharply.

Needless to say, these scenarios were usually pure fantasy. In *The Mystery of Moral Re-Armament,* Tom Driberg cites numerous examples of MRA's false claims. One example is a claim made at the January 16, 1952 MRA "Assembly of the Americas" in Miami, Florida, where a British delegate, "Bill Birmingham, Union Secretary of the Mosley Common Pit, Lancashire," stated that because of MRA activity at the mine "production had increased from 11-1/2 tons to 15 tons per man per shift," while wages had increased from 37 to 52 shillings per day. According to figures from Lord Robens, Chairman of the National Coal Board (which oversees all mine operations in Britain), production had actually increased from 2110 *pounds* per man in 1947 to 2190 *pounds* per man in 1952, while wages increased from 27 shillings 6 pence to 38 shillings per day.[23]

But fallacious claims of successful interventions in labor disputes were nothing new to the Buchmanites. More than a decade before the Miami Assembly, even *Time* magazine had seen fit on two occasions to make snide comments about Oxford Group Movement/MRA false claims in the labor-dispute field.[24]

Despite the exaggerated and often wholly unrealistic claims made by MRA, Buchman's movement did have some influence in the upper echelons of the labor bureaucracy. MRA publicly bragged of this influence: "Illustrations of the effectiveness of this ideology in industry could be taken from all around the world. One of the 'five giants of American labor' lay dying. [MRA never identifies the "giant."] He said to a Senator, 'Tell America that when Frank Buchman changed John Riffe [Executive Vice-President of the CIO], he saved American industry 500 million dollars.'"[25] In April 1953, 13 years after he fell under Buchman's influence, Riffe listed his aims for American labor. One of them sounded as if it could just as easily have been issued by a leader of a Nazi or Soviet official trade union: "With the united strength of labor and industry to back the government in a foreign policy that will win all nations."[26]

MRA's focus on labor was but one part of its post-war strategy to present Moral Re-Armament as the *only* alternative to Communism. In *Ideology and Co-Existence*—a Moral Re-Armament pamphlet distributed by the millions in 1959 in the U.S. and Britain—the anonymous MRA author states: "There are two ideologies bidding for the world today. One is Moral Re-Armament...; the other is Communism..."[27] This is a rather grandiose self-assessment, but hardly a surprising one from an organization whose members and leadership believed that it was guided directly by God.

One ideological prong of MRA's post-war strategy was its emphasis on influencing organized labor; the other two prongs were a McCarthyite brand of anti-Communism and crude homophobia. The Buchmanites could not conceive of anyone disagreeing with them, much less attacking them, unless he or she were under Communist influence or otherwise morally tainted—a fact abundantly obvious from reading their literature of the period. One 1950s Moral Re-Armament book states: "Moral Re-Armament cannot be honestly opposed on intellectual grounds because it is basic truth... opposition to Moral Re-Armament has special significance. It always comes from the morally defeated."[28] Like many other MRA pronouncements, this statement is very arrogant, but hardly surprising. MRA believed (like many deranged murderers—"God told me to do it") that it had a direct line to God, and hence *The* Truth; and who but someone morally tainted would oppose God's chosen representative? This is the cardinal article of faith in every religious fanatic's creed: s/he has *The* Truth, and anyone who criticizes that Truth, or its bearer, *must* be immoral.

MRA really did believe that there was a Communist under every bed (and a "pervert" in it). In *Ideology and Co-Existence* we read that,

"Chiang Kai-Shek was sold out and the mainland and Manchuria lost to Red China. . . Men, later found to be giving the Communist Party line, were successful with their deceptions and achieved the change of direction in American policy [which led to the "loss" of China]."[29] This is a clear echo of the charges of Joe McCarthy and the "China Lobby" that the State Department was filled with Communists who "sold out" Chiang Kai-Shek.

An even clearer echo of McCarthy—but in reference to homosexuals, "security risks" in MRA terms—can be found in a book written by Peter Howard, Buchman's successor as head of MRA, which was published a few years after *Ideology and Co-Existence*: "At one point, 264 homosexuals were reported to have been purged from the American State Department. Many of them moved from Washington to New York and took jobs in the United Nations. . ."[30] This startling information appears in a chapter titled "Queens and Queers." It's very reminiscent of Joe McCarthy's famous speech in Wheeling, West Virginia on February 9, 1950, in which he said: "I have here in my hand a list of 205—a list of names that were made known to the Secretary of State as being members of the Communist Party and who are, nevertheless, still working and shaping policy in the State Department." (Despite repeated challenges, McCarthy, of course, never produced the "list.") Another example of Buchmanite homophobia can be found in a 1963 advertisement in the *New York Times* in which Moral Re-Armament attacked "sexual deviants in high places who protect potential spies."[31]

MRA's attacks on homosexuals were not always purely venomous; at times they were also ludicrous. A 1954 Moral Re-Armament tract instructs readers on ways to spot homosexuals:

> "There are many who wear suede shoes who are not homosexual, but in Europe and America the majority of homosexuals do. They favor green as a color in clothes and decorations. Men are given to an excessive display and use of the handkerchief. They tend to let the hair grow long, use scent and are frequently affected in speech, mincing in gait and feminine in mannerisms. They are often very gifted in the arts. They tend to exhibitionism. They can be cruel and vindictive, for sadism usually has a homosexual root. They are often given to moods.
> ". . . There is an unnecessary touching of hands, arms and shoulders. In the homosexual the elbow grip is a well-known sign."[32] [33]

Frank Buchman died in Germany on August 6, 1961 and his long-time disciple, Peter Howard, took the reins of Moral Re-Armament.

MRA continued much as it had under Buchman for the next few years, but the loss of its guru was a blow from which the movement never recovered. Howard died suddenly in 1965 without designating a successor, and the organization quickly shriveled.

The leadership vacuum and the unsavory reputation Moral Re-Armament had acquired through its red-baiting and gay-baiting evidently combined to nearly put an end to MRA. By 1970 the organization had effectively ceased to exist in the U.S.[34]; and by 1972 it was in serious decline in Britain. At that point, its reputation was so tarnished that the liberal Protestant weekly, *The Christian Century*, reported that MRA, through its actions, had acquired "a sinister mafia image, and to be identified with it in any way remains a serious liability for anyone seeking public support."[35] At present, Moral Re-Armament continues to exist in both Britain and the U.S., but only as a shadow of its former self. (A few MRA books have been published over the last two decades, and MRA currently publishes a slick, expensively produced monthly magazine, *For a Change;* but MRA has been out of the public spotlight for decades and its membership is undoubtedly quite low.)

In the U.S., Moral Re-Armament lived on in the form of Up with People!, the cloyingly wholesome kiddie vocal group cum traveling pep rally whose "message" was, and is, taken straight from MRA. For the last quarter-century, Up with People! performances have been inflicted upon many millions of high school students (including the author on one dreary afternoon in the late 1960s).

Up with People! was founded in 1965 by MRA member J. Blanton Belk, and for its first two years was sponsored by MRA and the Reader's Digest Foundation. It was almost certainly intended to be MRA's "antidote to hippies and peaceniks," as the Dallas *Times Herald* put it in 1967. The group's formal ties with Moral Re-Armament were, however, shortlived. Following its incorporation in 1968, Up with People! became organizationally independent of Moral Re-Armament, though MRA's influence was, and still remains, obvious. One area in which that influence is evident is in Up with People!'s inflated self-concept. Calvin Trillin archly commented, "Any place that 'Up with People!' has visited tends to sound like a battleground in the struggle. . . the show always seems to have arrived in a foreign country 'just weeks after violent demonstrations'; the names of Negro urban areas are normally preceded by 'the streets of,' so that cast members talk of having sung in 'the streets of Watts.'"[36]

In 1990, Up with People!'s annual budget was $19 million, much of it contributed by corporations such as General Electric, Coca-

Cola, and Volvo. Members of the cast and their sponsors (often Rotary Clubs or the like) kicked in the rest. In 1990, cast members were expected to pay $9,200 for the privilege of being in the group for one year, though more than 30 percent of them received financial help from the organization.[37] In all likelihood, Up with People! will be around for some time, as the messages in its songs are music to corporate ears.

Today, Frank Buchman, the Oxford Groups, and Moral Re-Armament have been virtually forgotten. Probably not one person in a hundred under the age of 40 would recognize Buchman's name or the names Oxford Group Movement or Moral Re-Armament; and probably not one in a thousand could provide even the most meager information about Buchman or his groups.

But the influence of Frank Buchman and his minions lingers on. His doctrines are almost certainly more widely adhered to and more influential now than they ever were during his lifetime — even if not one person in a thousand knows their origin.

---

1. *The Mystery of Moral Re-armament*, by Tom Driberg. New York: Alfred A. Knopf, 1965. Quoted on page 37.
2. *The Oxford Group, Its History and Significance*, by Walter Houston Clark. New York, Bookman Associates, 1951. p. 41. The source given for this information is an unnamed alumnus.
3. Ibid., p. 49.
4. "Report on Buchmanism," *Time*, Jan. 4, 1943, p. 68.
5. *Time*, April 20, 1936, p. 37.
6. Driberg, op. cit., p. 256.
7. *The Confusion of Tongues*, by Charles W. Ferguson. Grand Rapids, MI: Zondervan Publishing House, 1940, p. 106.
8. Ibid.
9. Writers sympathetic to Buchman, the Oxford Group Movement and Alcoholics Anonymous have put a different interpretation on these events. A good example is provided by Bill Pittman in *A.A. The Way It Began*. In his carefully sanitized chapter on the Oxford Groups, Pittman omits mention of Buchman's comments to Hibden but notes that Buchman "claimed that the problem at Princeton was that most of the criticism of the Group's frankness on sexual matters came from a group of sexual perverts." (pp. 118-119) And he lets the matter rest with that.
10. *Saints Run Mad*, by Marjorie Harrison. London: John Lane The Bodley Head, 1934. Quoted on page 39.
11. "Report on Buchmanism," *Time*, Jan. 4, 1943, p. 68.
12. "Apostle to the Twentieth Century," by Henry P. Van Dusen, *The Atlantic Monthly*, July, 1934, p. 13.
13. Driberg, op. cit., p. 174.

14. Quoted in *The Groups Movement*, by the Most Rev. John A. Richardson. Milwaukee: Morehouse Publishing Co., 1935, pp. 23-24.

15. Quoted in Driberg, op. cit., p. 175.

16. Ibid.

17. Quoted in Driberg, pp. 68-69. The full interview is reprinted on pp. 68-71.

18. *Pass It On.* New York: Alcoholics Anonymous World Services, 1989, pp. 170-171.

19. Half a century later, MRA writer Garth Lean, in his *On the Tail of a Comet: The Life of Frank Buchman* (Colorado Springs: Helmer & Howard, 1988, p. 240), denied that Buchman had said "Thank God for Hitler." (It should be noted that this is not the wording in the interview, nor, to the best of my knowledge, is Buchman's statement quoted in this form in any source except Lean's book.) Lean quotes a fellow MRA member, Garrett Stearly, who was supposedly present at the interview, as stating that Buchman "said that Germany needed a new Christian spirit, yet one had to face the fact that Hitler had been a bulwark against Communism there—and you could at least thank heaven for that," a remark which Stearly regarded as "No eulogy of Hitler at all." Given the nature of journalism, it is certainly possible that the phrasing of Buchman's statement was that quoted by Stearly rather than that quoted in the *World Telegram* interview. In either case, however, it's quite clear that Buchman was happy that Hitler's rise to power had created a "front-line of defense" or a "bulwark" against Communism.

In his defense of Buchman, Lean makes no denial that Buchman waxed enthusiastic over the possibilities of a "God-controlled Fascist dictator." Indeed, it would be very surprising if Buchman didn't harbor such sentiments. The main thrust of Buchmanism was to persuade "key men" to place themselves under "God-control," so that they could carry out "God's will"; and there is virtually no one in a more "key" position than a fascist dictator.

20. "A God-Guided Dictator," *The Christian Century*, September 9, 1936, p. 1183.

21. Driberg, op. cit., pp. 64-65.

22. For a fuller description of these events see Driberg, op. cit., pp. 105-111. See also Clark, op. cit., p. 81; *Drawing Room Conversion: A Sociological Account of the Oxford Group Movement*, by Allan W. Eister. Durham, North Carolina: Duke University Press, 1950, pp. 62-63; "Less Buchmanism," *Time*, Nov. 24, 1941, pp. 59-60; and "Buchman's Kampf," *Time*, Jan. 18, 1943, pp. 65-66.

23. Driberg, op. cit., pp. 127-128.

24. See *Time*, Nov. 24, 1941, p. 59, and July 31, 1939, p. 34.

25. *Ideology and Co-Existence.* Moral Re-Armament, 1959, p. 14.

26. Ibid.

27. Ibid., p. 1.

28. *Remaking Men*, by Paul Campbell and Peter Howard. New York: Arrowhead Books, 1954, p. 66.

29. *Ideology and Co-Existence*, op. cit., p. 23.

30. *Britain and the Beast*, by Peter Howard. London: Heinemann, 1963, p. 47.

31. Quoted by Calvin Trillin in *The New Yorker*, December 16, 1967, p. 134.

32. Campbell and Howard, op. cit., pp. 60-62.

33. Given the virulent homophobia exhibited by the Oxford Groups/Moral Re-Armament, it seems fair to point out that the organization's founder, Frank Buchman, exhibited many signs of being a "closet case": 1) He never married; 2) It was never even hinted in any of the numerous books and magazine articles written about him and his movement that he had sexual relations with women; 3) He was obsessed with sexual "sin," specifically self-"abuse" and "perversion"; 4) From the time he was ordained in his early 20s until he was nearly 50, his primary concern was working

with young men; 5) He apparently relished discussing intimate sexual matters with young men; 6) He was markedly homophobic, which is often a defense mechanism used by "closet cases" to conceal their true desires from both themselves and others.

34. See "Moral Re-Armament RIP" in *National Review*, October 20, 1970, p. 1099.

35. "When the White Begins To Fade," *The Christian Century*, June 28, 1972, p. 704.

36. Trillin, op. cit., p. 132.

37. "1960s Troupe Celebrates 25 Years of Enthusiasm," by Dirk Johnson. *New York Times*, July 29, 1990, p. 18, section 1.

3

A Brief History of A.A.

The purpose of this chapter is *not* to give a detailed history of Alcoholics Anonymous. A.A.'s story has been told at length by other writers in other books.[1] The purpose of *Alcoholics Anonymous: Cult or Cure?* is to analyze A.A. as it exists today, and while readers will require a certain amount of historical information in order to understand A.A., they will not require an intimate knowledge of A.A. history. So, this chapter will provide an overview of A.A.'s history while emphasizing facts pertinent to its organizational development and the development of its "program."

William Griffith (Bill) Wilson, the co-founder and the driving force behind Alcoholics Anonymous, was born on November 24, 1895 in East Dorset, Vermont. His father, Gilman, a heavy drinker, was the foreman at a marble quarry. In 1905 his parents divorced, and Bill and his sister were entrusted to the care of their maternal grandparents while their mother studied osteopathy in Boston. Bill's grandfather was a landlord with extensive holdings and the richest man in East Dorset, so, despite the trauma of his parents' divorce and his separation from both his father and mother, Bill was at least materially well off during his late childhood and adolescence.

In 1917, following an unsuccessful attempt to get into MIT, Wilson joined the army and became a second lieutenant. He took his first drink that same year. On January 24, 1918 he married Lois Burnham, his sweetheart from Vermont, who remained his wife until he died in 1971. Later in 1918 he was shipped with his unit to Europe, though he never saw combat; and in 1919 he was shipped home, discharged, and began living in New York City.

Like many other returning veterans he had a tough time finding regular employment, and at one point he quit a job on the docks because he refused to join a union.[2] That's not surprising given Wilson's background, conservative politics, and admiration for businessmen — "power drivers" as he called them. (In the "Big Book" he comments that "Business and financial leaders were my heroes."[3]) In *Pass It On*, A.A.'s official Wilson biography, he's quoted as saying, "I objected very much to joining the union, and I was threatened by force, and I left the job rather than join the union."[4] Given the nature of the AFL unions, it wouldn't have been surprising if he was threatened. Eventually, Wilson landed a job as an investigator for a brokerage firm and began his rise on Wall Street, a rise which would make him a rich man and which would last until the stock market crash in 1929.

All through the 1920s, his drinking had gradually worsened, and when the crash came he went on a bender. He was ruined. He had been a margin trader and lost everything in the crash. Eventually he and Lois moved in with her father, she took a job in a department store, and his drinking continued to worsen. He couldn't hold a job and his drinking resulted in blackouts, bar room brawls, temporary separation from his wife, panhandling, DTs, and pawning household items to pay for booze. He was on the ropes physically and emotionally. In 1933 and 1934 he was hospitalized several times at the Charles B. Towns Hospital in Manhattan under the care of Dr. William Silkworth, with his brother-in-law, Leonard Strong, paying his hospital bills.

Bill Wilson finally escaped from his alcoholic nightmare at the end of 1934. In the fall of that year, Ebby T., an old boarding school friend, stopped by to visit him. Like Bill, Ebby had been an extremely heavy drinker, so Bill was quite surprised when Ebby refused to drink with him. When Bill asked him why, Ebby replied that he had gotten religion, and that he was a member of the evangelical Oxford Group Movement.

Ebby had been introduced to the Movement by Roland H., another alcoholic. Like Ebby, Roland was a "hopeless" alcoholic from a privileged background. Several years earlier he had been in desperate straits and had traveled to Switzerland and placed himself under the care of Dr. Carl Jung, the mystically inclined former pupil of Freud, in an attempt to find a cure for his alcoholism. Roland had been sober for a year while under Jung's direct care, but when he left Jung he had gotten drunk almost immediately. In frustration, Jung told him that his only chance lay in religious conversion, an option Roland had seized upon by joining the Oxford Groups. When

Roland told him about this way of overcoming alcoholism, Ebby had seized upon this "chance" as readily as had Roland.

Sitting in the Wilson kitchen, Ebby outlined the Groups' teachings to Wilson: 1) Admission of personal defeat; 2) Taking of personal inventory; 3) Confession of one's defects to another person; 4) Making restitution to those one has harmed; 5) Helping others selflessly; 6) Praying to God for the power to put these precepts into practice. Bill was unimpressed, however, and continued to drink for the next several weeks.

On December 11, 1934, Wilson's drinking came to a screeching halt. On that day he was readmitted to Towns Hospital, sedated, and subjected to Dr. Silkworth's "belladonna cure," a treatment regimen which included morphine and other psychoactive drugs in addition to belladonna (which in large doses is a powerful hallucinogen.[5] While under the influence of the "cure," Bill Wilson experienced his "spiritual awakening." He described the experience in *Alcoholics Anonymous Comes of Age:*

> "I found myself crying out, 'If there is a God, let Him show Himself! I am ready to do anything!'
>
> "Suddenly the room lit up with a great white light...All about me there was a wonderful feeling of Presence, and I thought to myself, 'So this is the God of the Preachers.'"[6]

The day after Bill Wilson's "spiritual awakening," Ebby T. brought him a copy of *The Varieties of Religious Experience*, by William James. Wilson read it cover to cover. He later wrote in the "Big Book" that he found the idea in it that spiritual experiences — which could come in many forms — had the power to transform lives. Nearly 20 years after he wrote the "Big Book," in *Alcoholics Anonymous Comes of Age*, he also credited James with the idea that "deflation at depth" was necessary before a spiritual experience could occur.[7] Curiously, neither the words "deflation at depth" nor the single word "deflation" occur anywhere in James' book; James does, however, state that some type of extremely jarring event often occurs before a "spiritual experience." Another important idea found in *Varieties*, and one which is the cornerstone of A.A., is the suggestion that the "only radical remedy ...for dipsomania is religiomania."[8]

For several months following his stay at Towns Hospital and his "spiritual awakening," Bill Wilson attempted to singlehandedly put Oxford Group principles into practice in the field of alcoholism. He worked tirelessly, seeking out drunks to "work on." He devoted all of his energies to attempts to help other alcoholics sober up — by carrying the Oxford Group Movement message to them — even to the point of allowing many to live in his home. All of his attempts ended in failure.

While Bill devoted his energies to fruitless attempts to sober up drunks, Lois continued to work in a department store. She wasn't making much money, and they were in a precarious financial position. Eventually Bill decided to seek employment, and in May 1935 he travelled to Akron, Ohio to take part in a proxy fight for control of a machine tool firm, the National Rubber Machinery Company. The fight went badly and Wilson quickly found himself alone in a hotel lobby with ten dollars in his pocket — and within a few feet of an inviting bar.

He didn't succumb to the temptation to seek companionship in such familiar surroundings; instead, he went to the nearest phone and called Walter Tunks, an Episcopalian minister and the leading supporter of the Oxford Groups among the Akron clergy. He told Tunks that he was a drunk and a member of the Oxford Groups who needed to find another drunk in order to stay sober. Tunks gave him ten numbers to call. After nine fruitless calls, he dialed the last number on the list, that of Henrietta Seiberling.

She was delighted to hear from Bill Wilson because she was very concerned about the destructive drinking of an Oxford Group friend, Dr. Robert Smith. Smith, a judge's son, was a Dartmouth graduate and an M.D. who had become a proctologist and skilled surgeon; but he was also a hardcore alcoholic with a disintegrating practice and severe financial problems. The day that Bill Wilson called Henrietta Seiberling, Smith was unavailable because he had passed out at home, dead drunk. So, Seiberling arranged for Wilson and Smith to meet late the following afternoon at her home.

Dr. Smith, who was very shaky that day, agreed to meet with Wilson only to please his wife Anne and his friend Henrietta. He expected to talk with the stranger from New York for no more than 15 minutes. They ended up talking for more than six hours, and Dr. Smith was deeply affected. The man who would later become known within A.A. as "Dr. Bob" immediately quit drinking.

Seeing the surprising change in her friend, Henrietta Seiberling was determined to keep Bill Wilson in Akron. At the time, however, Bill was dead broke; so, Henrietta arranged with a neighbor to allow Bill to stay at a local country club for two weeks. At about the same time, Bill received additional money from New York to continue the proxy fight over the machine tool company. After his two-week stay at the country club, he moved into the Smiths' home on the invitation of Anne Smith.

Wilson's stay at the Smiths' went smoothly. While he lived with them, Bill Wilson and the Smiths made the practice of Oxford Group principles a focus of their lives. In particular, they held a daily "quiet time" in the morning which they devoted to meditation, Bible reading, and receiving "guidance" from God. As importantly, Bill and Dr. Bob almost immediately began to "work on" other drunks.

Shortly after they began this regimen, Dr. Bob decided to attend the annual AMA convention in Atlantic City. Within a week of his leaving, he arrived back in Ohio blind drunk. Bill and Anne sobered him up, and on June 10, 1935, Dr. Bob took his last drink (to steady his nerves before an operation). This is often cited as the founding date of Alcoholics Anonymous.

Wilson and Smith wasted no time in continuing the search for other drunks. Despite several failures, they did succeed in sobering up two more alcoholics during the summer of 1935. By late that summer, however, the proxy fight for control of the machine tool company had failed, and Wilson was obliged to return to New York. He left behind him Dr. Smith and two other ex-drunks, all three of whom were attending Oxford Group meetings and faithfully practicing Oxford Group principles. Some time during or shortly after this period, Dr. Bob's small group of alcoholics started to call themselves "the alcoholic squadron [or "squad" — there are references to both names] of the Akron Oxford Group."

Once back in New York, Bill continued to devote most of his energies to working with other alcoholics, turning his home into a halfway house for drunks, again with no success. A particularly jarring failure was that of Bill C., a lawyer who lived with the Wilsons for almost a year. He committed suicide by sticking his head in the oven and turning on the gas. When Bill and Lois returned home following a visit to a member of their fledgling society in Maryland, they found Bill C.'s body and a house filled with gas.

In late 1935, at a time when the Wilson home still functioned as a halfway house, small groups of alcoholics and their wives began to meet there for an open house on Tuesday evenings; thus the second de facto A.A. group was born. It didn't take long for the Wilsons to notice that some of the drunks who turned up on Tuesday nights were staying sober, while none of those who were living in their de facto halfway house were managing to do so. The members of the Tuesday night group also attended Oxford Group meetings, a practice which would continue until late 1937. At that time the still-unnamed New York group of ex-alcoholics severed its connections with the Oxford Group Movement.

There were several reasons for the split. An important one was that Wilson and his band of ex-drunks were only interested in working with other alcoholics. As time went on, this caused friction with an ever-growing number of non-alcoholic Oxford Group members; increasing numbers of them received "guidance" that Wilson should quit working with alcoholics and instead concentrate his energies directly on Oxford Groups work. For their part, the alcoholics found the Oxford Groups too "authoritarian," and took no part in the Groups Movement other than attending meetings. From his writings, it seems clear that while Bill Wilson agreed wholeheartedly with Oxford Group Movement principles, he felt that for alcoholics, "These ideas had to be fed with teaspoons rather than by buckets."[9] (This statement largely explains why Oxford Group Movement principles are clearly presented, but are expressed so unforcefully, and at times euphemistically, in the "Big Book.")

These differences alone would probably have been enough to ensure the eventual disaffiliation of the reformed New York alcoholics from the Oxford Groups. It's also possible that Frank Buchman's interview in the August 26, 1936 *New York World Telegram* (discussed in Chapter 2), in which he was quoted as saying, "I thank heaven for a man like Adolf Hitler," provided additional incentive for Wilson to put distance between his group of ex-drunks and the Oxford Group Movement. That's impossible to know, however, as Bill Wilson apparently left no written record of the matter, and A.A.'s official literature treats it in a very circumspect manner.

There were two further reasons why Wilson's group left the Oxford Group Movement. One was that the Catholic Church was very critical of the Buchmanites, and Wilson didn't want to run the risk of Catholics being forbidden to join his group. The other was that the easiest way to avoid controversy and divisiveness was to concentrate solely on alcoholism. So, formal ties were severed between Wilson's ex-alcoholics and the Oxford Groups; nevertheless, the New Yorkers continued to be guided by many of the Oxford Group Movement's principles.

In the fall of 1937, Bill Wilson made a second business trip to Akron. While there he met with Dr. Smith. By this time, Wilson had decided that their organization needed to expand through paid missionaries, hospitals for alcoholics, and publication of its principles in book form, and that they needed to raise funds for those purposes. While he supported the idea of a book, Dr. Bob had doubts about paid missionaries and hospitals. Nevertheless, he supported all of Wilson's proposals at a meeting of the Akron "alcoholic squadron" and all of Bill's ideas were approved by a narrow margin after heated debate. Upon returning home, his proposals were enthusiastically approved by the New York group.

In the spring of 1938 Bill Wilson began to write what was to become the "Big Book" of Alcoholics Anonymous. After several months of work, Wilson completed the book. He apparently wrote the entire portion which outlined the A.A. program, with the exception of "The Doctor's Opinion," which was written by Dr. Wm. Silkworth of Towns Hospital. The remainder of the book consisted of members' stories. The New Yorkers wrote their own, while the Akronites composed theirs with the help of a member who had been a professional journalist. In addition to contributing their stories, members in New York and Akron read the sections Bill wrote and contributed criticisms and suggestions, many of which were incorporated into the book.

During the book's writing, serious disputes had arisen over both its title and contents. Before *Alcoholics Anonymous* was settled on as the title, several others had been proposed. One title in particular, *The Way Out*, was quite popular and would probably have been adopted but for the fact that there were 25 books listed by that name in the Library of Congress, while there were none listed under the name *Alcoholics Anonymous*.

More serious disagreement arose over the 12 Steps. They were a distillation of Oxford Group Movement principles, principles which some members of Wilson's New York group found unpalatable. In the original version of the Steps, Wilson had included the words "on our knees" in Step 7, but many members felt that this was too overtly religious and would drive away alcoholics. A few even objected to the use of the word "God," but they were outvoted. Some concessions, however, were made to nonbelievers — the elimination of the offending words in Step 7, the addition of the words "as we understood Him" after the word "God" in Steps 3 and 11, and the substitution of the phrase "a Power greater than ourselves" for the word "God" in Step 2. Additionally, the Steps were prefaced with the statement: "Here are the Steps we took which are suggested as a Program of Recovery." The changes made to the Steps were relatively insignificant, but the prefacing statement was important. Because it stated that A.A.'s "Program" was only "suggested," it (in theory) allowed nonbelievers to participate in A.A. without embracing the religiosity of the Steps.[10] (For a fuller discussion of the Steps, see Chapter 5.)

It's interesting to note that in the "Big Book" Bill Wilson gives no credit whatsoever to the Oxford Groups as the source of the A.A. program, even though every single one of the 12 Steps is directly traceable to Buchman's teachings. This deliberate omission was, almost certainly, the result of Wilson's desire not to incur the wrath of the Catholic clergy. The only influences he mentions in the "Big Book" are Carl Jung's advice to seek a cure for alcoholism through "vital spiritual experiences" and the idea expressed in William James' *Varieties of Religious Experience* that such experiences can take many forms.

A revealing sidelight to these attributions is that it's quite possible that Jung had borrowed the idea of "religiomania" as a cure for "dipsomania" directly from *Varieties*, which had been translated into German in 1907. What's even more revealing is the fact that the suggestion in James' book that religion could be cure for drunkenness had come directly from William S. Hadley, an American alcoholic who underwent his own "conversion experience" in New York City in 1871 and then immersed himself in evangelical missionary work — thus placing himself as a spiritual ancestor of the later evangelist and missionary, Frank Buchman.[11] So, it certainly seems possible that the idea of "religiomania" as a cure for "dipsomania" came full circle: from New York evangelist William Hadley to William James, from James to Carl Jung, and from Jung, via Roland and Ebby, to Bill Wilson back in New York, who failed to credit the immediate evangelical source of A.A.'s "program" (the Oxford Groups), while pointedly mentioning both Jung and James. Whatever the case, it seems probable that Wilson cited Jung and James in the "Big Book" in an attempt to lend it intellectual respectability, and that he failed to cite the Oxford Groups in order to avoid trouble with the Catholic Church.

While the "Big Book" was being written, Bill and his fellow A.A.'s moved to set up a formal non-profit organization to unify the fellowship and to enable the wealthy to give tax-deductible donations to it. The name they settled upon was the Alcoholic Foundation, and in May 1938 it held its first meeting. Its trustees (now the General Service Board of Alcoholics Anonymous) were divided between alcoholics and nonalcoholics, with the nonalcoholics holding a majority of one vote on the board.

The first steps toward obtaining financial backing from the rich were made in late 1937. Through his brother-in-law, Leonard Strong, Bill was able to see Willard Richardson, an ordained minister and an aide to John D. Rockefeller, Jr. Richardson arranged a meeting between Bill, Dr. Bob and other A.A. members, and several friends and advisers of Mr. Rockefeller. The meeting went smoothly, and one Rockefeller adviser, Frank Amos, was appointed to further investigate A.A. After traveling to Akron and observing Dr. Bob and company in action, Amos recommended that Rockefeller give $50,000 to A.A., with more to follow. Rockefeller, however, refused, citing the fear that "money will spoil this thing."[12] He did, however, donate $5000 to relieve Bill's and Dr. Bob's immediate financial problems. A portion of the money was used to pay off Dr. Smith's home mortgage, and the remainder was put in a trust fund from which A.A.'s two co-founders began to draw $30 per week apiece.

While Bill Wilson was writing the "Big Book," it was still unclear who would publish the book once it was finished. Wilson had received a contract offer with provision for a $1500 advance from a commercial publisher, Harper & Brothers, but after much contemplation — he was in serious financial straits despite Rockefeller's gift, and $1500 was a lot of money in 1938 — he decided, to his credit, that A.A. should publish its own literature.

The Alcoholic Foundation, however, did not raise any money for the project. So, Wilson and Hank P., another member of the New York A.A. group, set up an ad hoc publishing venture, Works Publishing Co. They expected to sell shares to the by now 50 or so A.A. members, but to their surprise and disappointment, they were unable to sell a single share. Finally, after they had talked to a member of the *Reader's Digest* staff and believed that they had obtained a promise of a story upon publication of the book, they managed to sell 200 shares at $25 each and Charles Towns lent them an additional $2500. Even so, they were still short of the funds necessary to print the book, and they would have had great difficulty in getting it published but for a sympathetic printer, with apparently deep pockets, who agreed to print an initial run with no guarantee other than Bill's and Hank's promise of eventual payment. Finally, in April 1939, the "Big Book" was published with a press run of 5,000 copies. At the time A.A. had only about 100 members.

While Bill Wilson was busy in New York attempting to sober up drunks, hauling them to Oxford Group meetings, attempting to raise money, founding the Alcoholic Foundation and Works Publishing Co., and writing what was to become the "Big Book," Dr. Bob was busy in Akron attending to the day-to-day business of searching out and sobering up drunks. The usual procedure was for Dr. Smith and the other reformed drunks to visit a hospitalized alcoholic, give him the "facts" on alcoholism, tell their stories, and ask him if he wanted to quit drinking and was willing to do what was necessary to stop. If he was, Dr. Bob would make him get out of bed, get on his knees, and "surrender" to God. Those who for some reason were not hospitalized were forced at their first Oxford Group meeting to go to an upstairs room with Dr. Bob and the other reformed alcoholics and to "surrender" before they were allowed to participate.

In those days, hospitalization for upwards of a week was the normal practice in Akron. Dr. Bob customarily prescribed it even for alcoholics who had no physical need of it, in order that they be isolated and thus have time to contemplate their situation and to be properly "worked on." The only reading material they were allowed was the Bible. By making hospitalization a routine practice, Dr. Bob's group quickly ran up huge hospital bills, even though (unbelievable as it may seem to present-day readers) the daily cost of hospitalizing a patient then was less than the cost of an expensive hotel room.

A notable practice of the reformed alcoholics in Akron at this time (and, shortly after, in Cleveland as well), was that Dr. Smith and his band aggressively pursued prospects. Besides dropping in uninvited on hospitalized alcoholics, they would call on alcoholics at their homes in order to explain their program and to try to recruit them. Clarence S., the founder of A.A. in Cleveland, is even reported to have hauled prospects off barstools. This is in marked contrast to A.A.'s present approach: A.A. has now abandoned its early practice of aggressively pursuing prospects in order to *persuade* them to join, and instead presents a "take it or leave it" posture to the public while it simultaneously cooperates with treatment programs and traffic courts which *force* patients and convicted drunk drivers to attend A.A. meetings.

In early 1937, alcoholics from Cleveland began to make the trip to Akron in order to attend Oxford Group meetings with Dr. Bob and the other Akron alcoholics. Their numbers gradually grew, and by early 1939 they had decided to start meeting in Cleveland. Many of them were Catholics, which was probably the key consideration in their decision to not only begin meeting in Cleveland, but to meet separately from the Oxford Groups. This provoked a minor furor, as many of the alcoholic members of the Akron Oxford Group felt betrayed; but they followed the Clevelanders out of the Oxford Groups by the end of the year. For their name, the Cleveland alcoholics chose the name of the just-published "Big Book": Alcoholics Anonymous. They thus became the first group to officially use the A.A. name.

The "Big Book" was well received in the popular and religious press, but not in the scientific or medical press. It received a favorable review in *The New York Times*, and several religious publications printed a glowing review written by the influential clergyman, Dr. Harry Emerson Fosdick. The book received scant notice in medical and scientific publications, however, other than a scathing review in the October 14, 1939 *Journal of the American Medical Association* which charged that the book "is a curious combination of organizing propaganda and religious exhortation. It is in no sense a scientific book. . . ." The reviewer went on to say, "The book contains instructions as to how to intrigue the alcoholic addict into the acceptance of divine guidance in place of alcohol in terms strongly reminiscent of Dale Carnegie and the adherents of the Buchman ('Oxford') movement. The one valid thing in the book is the recognition of the seriousness of addiction to alcohol. Other than this, the book has no scientific merit or interest."

Despite Dr. Fosdick's enthusiastic and widely published review, very few copies of the "Big Book" sold initially. The *Reader's Digest* article, which Bill Wilson and the other A.A. members had been counting on so heavily, never appeared, and spirits were at a low ebb until one of the New York members, Morgan R., managed to arrange a three-minute interview on a national radio show. On April 25, 1939 he appeared on Gabriel Heatter's "We the People" program. The interview went well, and Bill and the other early A.A.'s sat back and waited for orders for the book to pour in. To stimulate demand, they had raised $500 and had used the money to mail promotional postcards announcing the broadcast and the book to every physician east of the Mississippi River. Three days after the broadcast they arrived at the post office, empty suitcases in hand, to reap what they expected would be a harvest of hundreds if not thousands of orders for the "Big Book." They were rudely surprised. They received a total of 12 replies, with only two of them being book orders.

Further publicity quickly rescued A.A. from the depression induced by the postcard fiasco. In June, the *New York Times* ran its favorable review of *Alcoholics Anonymous*, and shortly thereafter *Liberty* magazine, a popular national weekly, published an article lauding A.A. The article, titled "Alcoholics and God" and written by Morris Markey, appeared in *Liberty*'s September 30, 1939 issue. The New York A.A.s weren't especially happy with the piece because of its title, its emphasis on the religious nature of A.A., and Markey's explanation of 12th-Step work: "These men were experiencing a psychic change. Their so-called 'compulsion neurosis' was being altered—transferred from liquor to something else. Their psychological necessity to drink was being changed to a psychological necessity to rescue their fellow victims from the plight that made them so miserable."[13] Still, the Markey article did lead to 800 inquiries—most of them from the South and overtly religious, according to one chronicler[14]—and resulted in a burst of book sales, growth, and, eventually, the formation of A.A.'s first "mail order" group in Little Rock, Arkansas. A.A.'s final stroke of luck in 1939 was the publication of a series of highly laudatory articles in the *Cleveland Plain Dealer*. The articles led to a spurt of growth in Cleveland and surrounding areas, and Cleveland-area A.A.s quickly outnumbered those in Akron and New York combined.

That was a temporary situation, as within two years A.A. would receive its most important publicity boost, and its effects would dwarf those of everything previously published or broadcast about A.A.; it was responsible in large part for A.A.'s transformation into a nationwide movement. On March 1, 1941, the *Saturday Evening Post*, then one of the most important magazines in the country, published Jack Alexander's article "Alcoholics Anonymous" (with the subhead "Freed Slaves of Drink, Now They Free Others"). It generated an avalanche of responses and, according to A.A.'s own estimate, 6,000 new members.[15] The article was so laudatory and so important to A.A. history that A.A. subsequently reprinted it and still distributes it as a pamphlet.

In June of the same year, while perusing the obituary column in the *Herald Tribune*, a New York A.A. discovered a short incantation which in the following years would be repeated millions of times at A.A. meetings, The Serenity Prayer: "God grant me the serenity to accept the things I cannot change, the courage to change the things I can, and the wisdom to know the difference." The prayer is often credited to the Protestant theologian, Reinhold Niebuhr. If he did write it, there's more than a trace of irony in the fact that the author of this prayer which is so much a part of A.A. had acidly attacked A.A.'s spiritual father, Frank Buchman, because of Buchman's pro-Hitler remarks in 1936.[16]

While A.A. was rapidly growing as a result of all the free publicity it was receiving, its co-founders' financial problems were finally being resolved. Despite the $30-a-week stipend from the Rockefeller money, the early years of A.A. were a financially disastrous period for Bill Wilson. In 1939 the mortgage company which held the title to Lois' father's house evicted them and sold the building. They were homeless for the next two years. When Bill was asked at some later date how he and Lois had survived that period, he reportedly replied, "We were invited out to dinner a lot."

Their fortunes took a turn for the better in 1940. Early that year, the Alcoholic Foundation trustees, at Bill's urging, had decided that A.A. itself should own the rights to the "Big Book." The foundation soon managed to acquire all of the stock in Works Publishing, and its trustees had voted to pay both Bill and Dr. Bob royalties on book sales. As sales increased, those royalties became substantial enough that Bill was able to drop his sporadic attempts to obtain outside employment, and to devote all of his energies to A.A. In November 1940, after well over a year of being the guests of various A.A.s, Bill and Lois moved into a small room in the first A.A. clubhouse, a small building on 24th Street in New York City. Six months later they moved into their own home. It was in Bedford Hills, in expensive Westchester County, but they were able to buy it because its owner was willing to sell it to them for $6,500 with no money down and payments of $40 a month.

Dr. Bob's financial condition had been desperate before the 1938 Rockefeller donation, and even after his mortgage was paid off and he began to receive his stipend, he was still in bad financial shape. He was devoting most of his time to A.A. work, and his practice, though gradually recovering, was still poor. As the 1940s progressed, however, his practice improved, and the income from it and the ever-increasing royalties from "Big Book" sales allowed him to spend the final years of his life in relative comfort.

The early years of World War II would have been quite difficult for him and for Bill Wilson, though, if Rockefeller hadn't once again lent a helping hand. In early 1940 Willard Richardson, now a member of the Alcoholic Foundation's board of trustees, revealed that John D. Rockefeller, Jr. wanted to hold a dinner for A.A. to which he would invite a large number of his wealthy friends. It was held on February 8, 1940 at New York City's Union Club. Of the 400 guests Rockefeller had invited, 75 showed up. They were treated to speeches by Bill, Dr. Bob, Harry Emerson Fosdick, and Dr. Foster Kennedy. Rockefeller was sick that evening, so he was unable to attend and his son, Nelson, delivered the after-dinner summation. He reiterated his father's sympathetic interest in A.A., and then added, "Gentlemen, you can all see that this is a work of good will. Its power lies in the fact that one member carries the good message to the next, without any thought of financial income or reward. Therefore it is our belief that Alcoholics Anonymous should be self-supporting so far as money is concerned. It needs only our good will."[17] And with that, the guests applauded, shook hands with the assembled A.A.s, and filed out into the night.

Bill, Dr. Bob, and the other A.A.s were extremely disappointed, but John D. Jr. did end up giving them some assistance. Shortly after the dinner, he donated $1000 to A.A., bought 400 copies of the "Big Book," and sent them, along with a letter hinting that A.A. needed additional financial help, to all 400 persons to whom he had sent invitations. They responded by donating $2000, and would continue to contribute a similar amount annually for the next four years. John D. also had his publicists, in conjunction with A.A., draft a press release which generated a considerable amount of favorable publicity for Alcoholics Anonymous.

Thanks largely to the free publicity it was receiving, A.A. grew rapidly during the opening days of World War II. When the "Big Book" was published in 1939, A.A. had two groups (one in Akron, one in New York), a membership of no more than 100, and no national office. Two-and-a-half years later, in the final days of 1941, A.A. had 200 groups, a membership of 8,000, and a national office in New York City.[18] By 1944, A.A. had 360 groups with a total membership of 10,000, and in June of that year had begun publication of what was to become its official organ, *The Grapevine*, which had originally been a newsletter for A.A.s in the armed forces.

In October of that year there was a second significant development. The National Committee for Education on Alcoholism (NCEA, later the National Council on Alcohol, now the National Council on Alcoholism and Other Drug Addictions—NCA for short) opened its first office. Marty Mann, the first woman to achieve lasting sobriety in A.A., was its founder, and both Bill Wilson's and Dr. Bob's *full* names appeared on its letterhead as sponsors. This caused a storm of controversy within A.A. in 1946, when the NCEA mailed a fundraising appeal on its letterhead stationery, with some copies of the appeal going to A.A. groups. The names of Bill and Dr. Bob quickly vanished from the letterhead.[19] Since then, great care has been taken to avoid any formal ties between A.A. and the NCA, though the NCA has certainly seemed to function as A.A.'s lobbying arm and spokesman on issues involving "public controversy." (The 10th Tradition forbids A.A. from involving itself in "public controversy.")

During this early period of growth, Bill Wilson was on the road a great deal of the time visiting members and groups scattered across the country. He also spent a lot of time at headquarters dealing with correspondence from A.A. groups and members, where he quickly noticed that many problems and questions recurred over and over again. In an attempt to formulate a set of guidelines to help groups deal with these recurring problems and questions, Bill wrote the 12 Traditions. Just as the 12 Steps were Bill's, and subsequently A.A.'s, principles for conduct of one's personal life, the 12 Traditions were Bill's principles for the conduct of A.A.'s organizational life. They were first published in the April 1946 *Grapevine*; and, strange as it now seems, they were not universally well received within A.A. Bill Wilson spent a good part of the next few years on the road stumping for them before they were unanimously adopted by A.A.'s first international convention in 1950.

During the 1940s, both Bill and Dr. Bob were avidly pursuing a common interest outside of, but related to, A.A.: spiritualism. They believed that it demonstrated the existence of the "Higher Power" so central to the A.A. program. Thus, shortly after the Wilsons moved into their Bedford Hills home, they began to hold regular "spook sessions," complete with mysterious messages on a ouija board, and on at least one occasion they held a "spirit rapping" session (a seance in which spirits supposedly rap out messages with an "a" being one rap, a "b" two, a "c" three, etc., spirits evidently being too dense to learn the far more efficient Morse code).[20]

The 1940s were not, however, a uniformly happy time for A.A.'s co-founders. In 1944, despite his new home, newfound financial security, and A.A.'s continuing growth and increasing respectability, Bill Wilson fell into deep depression; it was a problem which would plague him for more than a decade. For Dr. Bob Smith, the 1940s brought tragedy. In 1948 he learned that he had incurable prostate cancer; in 1949 his wife Anne died; and in 1950 he too died following a prolonged, painful illness. He was buried next to his wife in an Akron cemetery. At his request, as a final expression of his dedication to the principle of anonymity, he had a simple gravestone which made no mention of Alcoholics Anonymous.

Despite his ongoing problems with depression, Bill Wilson was extremely active during this period. In addition to stumping for the 12 Traditions, he was also promoting a plan for A.A. to become self-governing. It says more than a little about his dedication to principles rather than personal aggrandizement that he devised the plan which would eventually make it impossible for him, or any other individual, to control A.A. Briefly, the plan called for A.A.'s affairs to be directed by a constituent assembly, called the General Service Conference, which would meet once a year and would be elected at area conferences. In turn, the delegates to the area conferences would be the elected representatives of the individual A.A. groups, the Group Service Representatives (GSRs), and the District Committee Members elected by the GSRs. To ensure continuity, delegates to the General Service Conference were to be elected to staggered terms, with approximately half being elected in even years and half elected in odd years, with terms of office running two years. The plan called for every state and Canadian province to have one delegate, with states and provinces with large numbers of A.A. members to have additional representation.

The plan was approved for a probationary five-year period at the 1950 international convention, and the first General Service Conference was held in New York in 1951. Only 37 delegates attended that first conference, but even so, it was considered an outstanding success. Following the conference's conclusion, Bill Wilson commented, "As I watched all this grow, I became entirely sure that Alcoholics Anonymous was at last safe — even from me."[21] An additional 38 delegates were elected to the conference the following year. In 1955, the second international A.A. convention declared that the General Service Conference plan had successfully completed its probationary period and was an accepted part of A.A. At present, delegates are still elected for staggered two-year terms, and there are now 91 delegates.

The year 1955 saw another significant development — publication of the second edition of the "Big Book." Except for a few minor changes, such as the elimination of the term "ex-alcoholic" and the substitution of the euphemism "illness" for "disease," very little was changed in the section written by Bill Wilson. The major changes made were in the section consisting of members' stories; several were added and several deleted to make the book more up to date.

Bill Wilson wrote two additional books in the 1950s. In 1953 A.A. published *12 Steps and 12 Traditions*, commonly called the "12 & 12," Wilson's at-length explication of the principles set forth in the Steps and Traditions. In 1957 A.A. published his *Alcoholics Anonymous Comes of Age*, which was Wilson's history and evaluation of A.A. up to the point where formal control was turned over to its members at the 1955 international convention.

There was one other development in the early and mid-'50s which, though not a part of A.A.'s organizational history, should be mentioned: The formation of the first non-A.A. groups which adopted the A.A. "program," especially the 12 Steps, with only minimal modifications. The first of these was Al-Anon, an organization for family members of alcoholics, which appeared in 1951.

The second was Alateen, a group for the teenage children of alco-holics, which appeared in 1957. In the years to come there would be literally hundreds of other A.A. spinoffs.

A.A. grew rapidly during the ten years following World War II. During the first few years, especially, A.A.'s membership mush-roomed. In 1951 A.A. had 112,000 members and 4,000 groups; and in 1955 A.A. had 132,00 members and nearly 6,000 groups.[22] In the years to come, A.A. would continue to grow very rapidly. By the end of 1957, A.A. had over 7,000 groups and 200,000 members scattered across 70 countries, but with the vast majority in the United States.[23] A.A. abroad, however, had sufficient numerical strength that the first overseas General Service Board of Alcoholics Anonymous was created in the U.K. and Ireland in that same year, 1957.

As a sign that A.A. had "come of age," Bill Wilson largely disengaged himself from the day-to-day administration of the General Service Office, A.A.'s national service center in New York. One indication of how much work he had been doing is that, following his disengagement, A.A. set up a Public Information Committee to take charge of the public relations work which Bill had formerly handled.

Shortly before the second international A.A. convention, Bill Wilson discovered a new interest — LSD. At the time it was con-sidered a promising therapeutic agent for the treatment of alcohol-ism, which is what aroused Bill's interest in it. He first took the drug in 1956 and was quite enthusiastic, believing that the drug had the ability to sweep away mental barriers which keep people from di-rectly experiencing the presence of God.[24] Secrecy was never one of Bill Wilson's strong points, and he soon had a coterie of friends and acquaintances, including clergymen and psychiatrists, joining him in his LSD experiments. Word of this traveled fast, and controversy soon followed, the nation being then, as now, in the grip of anti-drug hysteria. Even though initial studies involving LSD treatment of alcoholics had shown promising results, and the facts that LSD produced no physically damaging side effects and definitely was not addictive, the press was circulating sensational and wildly inaccurate reports of LSD's effects. So, because his name would inevitably be linked with A.A. even though he had formally withdrawn from its day-to-day administration, Bill Wilson ended his LSD experiments in 1959.[25]

In early 1961 Wilson wrote to Carl Jung, expressing his appreci-ation of Jung's influence (via Roland H.) in the forming of A.A. By chance, he had written just a few months before Jung's death. Jung replied with a gracious letter which became one of Wilson's treasured possessions.[26]

Just two months after Jung died, Frank Buchman, who had contributed far more to A.A. than had Jung, also died. Bill Wilson had never bothered to write to Buchman to express his thanks, and regretted that he had not done so. He commented in a letter to a friend: "Now that Frank Buchman is gone and I realize more than ever what we owe to him, I wish I had sought him out in recent years to tell him of our appreciation."[27]

At about the same time as his correspondence with Jung, Bill Wilson was developing another new interest: niacin (vitamin B-3) as a treatment for alcoholism. He believed that it was the long-sought-after cure for the "allergy" mentioned by Dr. Silkworth in the "Big Book." By the mid-1960s he was zealously promoting niacin to both the medical community and to the members of A.A. This, naturally enough, caused still another controversy, and in 1967 the A.A. General Service Board requested that he not use the General Service Office address on his stationery.

In that same year, A.A. published Bill Wilson's final book. Its original title was *The A.A. Way of Life*; it has since been retitled *As Bill Sees It*. The book is a collection of Wilson's writings, and resembles nothing so much as a prayer book, complete with a long ribbon at the top of its spine. *The A.A. Way of Life* marked Bill Wilson's last significant contribution to Alcoholics Anonymous. The year before it was published, the General Service Conference had finally approved, after years of dragging its heels, Wilson's plan to reverse the ratio of alcoholic to non-alcoholic trustees on A.A.'s board of directors, the General Service Board. Following the Conference's decision, the board's composition was reversed, and for the first time alcoholic members held a majority of the votes. When this was done, Bill felt that A.A. had finally become truly mature.

It was fortunate that Bill Wilson lived to see this change which he so fervently desired, as his health was rapidly failing during the late 1960s. Like Dr. Bob, Bill Wilson was a smoker, and by the late '60s he had developed emphysema, which caused him increasing pain and debilitation as the decade advanced. Still, even while his health deteriorated, he continued to smoke. He finally quit in 1969, but by then the damage had been done, and his last two years of life were plagued by tobacco-caused disease, debilitation, and misery. He did attend the A.A. international convention in Miami in 1970, but he barely managed to speak for four minutes. Finally, after a lingering bout of pneumonia, he died on January 24, 1971.

While Bill Wilson had been attempting to have the trustee ratio altered, promoting niacin, and overseeing production of his final book, A.A. was in a period of change and expansion. The 1960s saw significant A.A. growth overseas, and by 1967 20 percent of A.A. members lived outside of the United States.[28] A second trend in the '60s was that relatively large numbers of newcomers had drug problems in addition to alcohol problems. This eventually led to the formation of other 12-Step groups, such as Narcotics Anonymous, which cater to those whose problems are not primarily alcohol related. The final trend which became noticeable in the 1960s (though it had certainly been present in the 1950s) was the widespread incorporation of A.A. as an integral part of hospital and institutional alcoholism programs. In the 1970s and 1980s the trend toward internationalization continued, as did the trend toward new members having multiple "dependencies" (with the concomitant trend of new 12-Step organizations catering to those with different "dependencies") and the trend toward A.A. integration into hospital and institutional programs.

In the 1970s another trend emerged which deserves comment: the formation of "special meetings." These are A.A. meetings for members who share special interests or desires beyond overcoming alcoholism. Examples include lesbian and gay meetings, nonsmokers meetings, and atheists and agnostics meetings. No A.A. member is turned away from these special meetings, but when those not sharing a group's special interest show up, they are oftentimes advised that though they are welcome they might feel more comfortable at other meetings. This trend from the 1970s, as well as those begun in the 1960s, continued throughout the 1980s.

By 1990 fully half of A.A.'s worldwide membership of 1.8 million lived outside of the United States[29]; between 1977 and 1989 the percentage of A.A. members also addicted to drugs rose from approximately 19 percent to approximately 46 percent[30]; the number of 12-Step spinoff organizations is now estimated at 100, 200, and even higher; and, as I write, participation in A.A. is either a voluntary or mandatory aspect of virtually every institutional alcoholism program in the country.

In the last decade of the 20th century, A.A. is a mass organization, and one with great influence in both the United States and abroad. In June 1990, there were 43,107 A.A. groups in the U.S., with 896,033 members; and worldwide there were 87,696 groups with 1,793,834 members. The irony is that during its over 50 years of expansion and external changes, the core of A.A.'s program has remained virtually unchanged, and at present probably not one member in 100 of A.A. or other 12-Step groups has more than the foggiest concept of where the ideas contained in 12-Step programs originated.

---

1. Those interested in more detailed histories should consult *Alcoholics Anonymous Comes of Age*, by Bill Wilson; *Getting Better*, by Nan Robertson; *A.A. The Way It Began*, by Bill Pittman; *The Sober Alcoholic*, by Irving Peter Gellman; *Not God: A History of Alcoholics Anonymous* (later retitled, in an updated edition, *The A.A. Story*), by Ernest Kurtz; *Pass It On* (A.A.'s official Wilson biography); *Dr. Bob and the Good Oldtimers* (A.A.'s official Smith biography); *Bill W.*, by Robert Thomsen; and *The A.A. Service Manual*.

2. *Getting Better*, by Nan Robertson. New York: Wm. Morrow & Co., 1988, p. 41.

3. *Alcoholics Anonymous*, Third Edition, by Bill Wilson. New York: Alcoholics Anonymous World Services, Inc., 1985, p.2

4. *Pass It On*. New York: Alcoholics Anonymous World Services, 1984, p. 63.

5. For details of the "cure" see *A.A. The Way It Began*, by Bill Pittman. Seattle: Glen Abbey Books, 1988, pp. 163-169.

6. *Alcoholics Anonymous Comes of Age*, by Bill Wilson. New York: Alcoholics Anonymous World Services, 15th printing, 1989 p. 63

7. Ibid., p. 64.

8. *The Varieties of Religious Experience*, by William James. New York: New American Library, Inc., 1958, p.213 (footnote).

9. *Alcoholics Anonymous Comes of Age*, p. 75.

10. Ibid., pp. 166-167.

11. See "The Ideology of a Therapeutic Social Movement: Alcoholics Anonymous," by Leonard Blumberg in *Journal of Studies on Alcohol*, Vol. 38, November 1977, pp. 2122-2143.

12. *Alcoholics Anonymous Comes of Age*, p. 150.

13. "Alcoholics and God," by Morris Markey. *Liberty*, September 30, 1939, p. 7.

14. *Not God*, by Ernest Kurtz. Center City, Minnesota: Hazelden Educational Services, 1979, p. 284.

15. *Pass It On*, p. 249.

16. "Hitler and Buchman," by Reinhold Niebuhr in *The Christian Century*, October 7, 1936, p. 1315.

17. *Alcoholics Anonymous Comes of Age*, pp. 184-185.

18. Figures cited in A.A.'s conference-approved literature are seemingly at odds. In *Pass It On*, the figure cited is 6,000 members in November 1941 (p. 266); and in *Alcoholics Anonymous Comes of Age*, the figure given is 8,000 members "at the end of 1941" (p. 192). Considering the inherent difficulties in accurately estimating A.A. membership, especially at this early stage, this minor discrepancy isn't surprising.

19. *Pass It On*, p. 320.

20. Ibid., pp. 275-280.

21. *A.A. Service Manual*, p. S19.

22. *Pass It On*, pp. 344 & 358.

23. *Alcoholics Anonymous Comes of Age*, p. ix.

24. In this belief, he wasn't alone; those who have taken large amounts of LSD report that one of its most common effects is the sweeping away of ego barriers and a feeling of oneness with the universe.

25. See *Pass It On*, pp. 368-377 for fuller details of Wilson's LSD experimentation.

26. As mystically minded as ever, Jung, in his letter, contemptuously dismissed "mere rationalism," and stated, "An ordinary man, not protected by an action from above and isolated in society, cannot resist the power of evil, which is called very aptly the Devil." This seems less like an attempt at insight than an attempt to evade it. Jung's comments bring to mind Wilhelm Reich's caustic comment in *The Mass Psychology of Fascism* that, "Every form of mysticism is reactionary, and the reactionary man is mystical."

In regard to Hitler and Nazism, Jung's reactions were almost as naive as those of Frank Buchman, A.A.'s spiritual father. Jung was ambivalent about the rise to power of the Nazis, and he foolishly allowed himself to be used for propaganda purposes by the Nazi media. At a time when the mystical, anti-semitic, anti-union, militaristic, and police-state tendencies of the Nazis were already blindingly obvious, and after they had already set up the first concentration camps, Jung still didn't realize what Nazism meant. He willingly appeared on Berlin radio in June 1933 where a Nazi Jungian psychiatrist interviewed him and elicited comments about "times of leadership," "the aimless conversation of parliamentary delibera-tion," and the older generation's acquiescence "to this natural course of events." Jung's biographer, Gerhard Wehr, called this interview "a thoroughly shameful business." (*Jung: A Biography*, by Gerhard Wehr. Boston: Shambala, 1987, pp. 320-321). In a later article, Jung noted, "The ultimate outcome of this unmistakable mass movement [Nazism] still seemed to me uncertain, just as the figure of the Fuhrer at first struck me as being merely ambivalent." He also stated that because of the "archetypal" nature of the forces driving such "psychological mass movement[s]," "it is impossible to make out at the start whether it will prove to be positive or negative." (Quoted in *Jung's Last Years,* by Aniela Jaffe. Dallas, Texas: Spring Publications, 1984, pp. 79-80) Other observers—even though many labored under the handicap of utilizing "mere rationality"—had no such difficulty in determining whether the Third Reich would be a "positive or negative" development.

Those interested in meaningful analyses of Nazism and the reasons for its rise would do well to consult *The Mass Psychology of Fascism*, by Wilhelm Reich; *Fascism and Big Business*, by Daniel Guerin; and *The Irrational in Politics*, by Maurice Brinton.

27. Quoted in *Pass It On*, p. 387.

28. *Alcoholics Anonymous Comes of Age*, p. x.

29. Information provided by General Service Board of Alcoholics Anonymous on June 5, 1990.

30. "Comments on A.A.'s Triennial Surveys," 1990, p. 10, figure B-2.

4

The Oxford Groups & A.A.: Similarities & Differences

"Our debt to them [the Oxford Group Movement]...was and is immense."
— Bill Wilson in *Alcoholics Anonymous Comes of Age*, p. 73

It would be surprising if anyone who read the preceding chapters didn't notice certain similarities between Alcoholics Anonymous and the Oxford Groups, for there are similarities in abundance in terms of ideology, operation, and style.

A.A. took its central doctrines virtually without change from Frank Buchman's Oxford Group Movement. This can be seen clearly in the 12 Steps, the cornerstone of A.A.'s program. The following chapter is devoted entirely to the 12 Steps, so for now suffice it to say that the Buchmanite principles of *personal powerlessness* and the necessity of *divine guidance* are embodied in Steps 1, 2, 3, 6, 7 & 11; the principle of *confession* is embodied in Steps 4, 5 & 10; the principle of *restitution* to those one has harmed is embodied in Steps 8 & 9; and the principle of *continuance*, of continuing to practice the other Buchmanite principles and to carry the word to other "defeated" persons ("alcoholics," in the Steps) so that they too will "change," is embodied in Steps 10 & 12.

To spell out some of these correspondences in more detail: A.A. inherited the Oxford Group Movement belief that human beings in themselves are powerless and that only submission to God's will is sufficient to solve human problems. It also inherited the belief that God will guide anyone who "listens." An additional Buchman legacy is the belief that it's necessary for human beings to confess their "wrongs" (in A.A.) or "sins" (in the Oxford Groups); as well, both groups employ(ed) both private and public confessions. The Oxford Groups emphasized private confessions from "sinners" to individual "soul surgeons," and public confessions at houseparties, while A.A. emphasizes private confessions from "pigeons" (newcomers being indoctrinated with the A.A. program) to "sponsors" (experienced members responsible for indoctrinating individual newcomers) and public confessions at A.A. meetings.

A closely related concept, common to both A.A. and the Oxford Groups, is belief in the necessity of "sharing." This term includes both private and public confession, but also encompasses giving "witness" both privately and publicly. In A.A., this concept is embedded in the twelfth Step in the injunction "to carry this message to alcoholics." While A.A. has for the most part dropped the term "sharing" (which is now usually associated with the brie and chablis set), it still adheres to it religiously.

Another point of ideological correspondence between the two organizations is that A.A., in exactly the same manner as the Oxford Groups, ignores social, political and economic factors as causes of personal and social problems. A.A. concerns itself solely with alcoholism (more properly, with its own program for alcoholics), but even though its focus is narrower than that of the Oxford Groups, its approach is identical. Nowhere in the dozens of books and pamphlets published by A.A. will you find even a hint that there is any cause of alcoholism (or even contributory factors) other than the alcoholic individual him (or her) self.

This extreme emphasis on individual responsibility rather than social factors, and the accompanying belief in the necessity of divine guidance, implies acceptance of the political-economic status quo and a marked disinterest in, and at times outright hostility to, political activism. Critics recognized this tendency in the Oxford Groups well *before* Bill Wilson and "Dr. Bob" joined the Oxford Group Movement and organized within it what was to become A.A.[1] In 1932, Frank Buchman expressed his anti-political activist attitude in as callous a manner as is imaginable. In that year when tens of millions were unemployed, with a very large number of them homeless and wandering the streets and highways, well-fed Frank Buchman stated: "The President's social trends report indicates there will surely be a revolution in this country. We are going to make it a spiritual revolution. What hunger marchers need is to be changed."[2] Buchman didn't say a word about food, housing, or employment; he knew what the hungry and poverty stricken *really* needed — divine guidance.

In present-day A.A., this anti-activist tendency is not as extreme as it was in the Oxford Groups, but it's still so obvious that observers who know next to nothing of A.A.'s history or that of its predecessor, the Oxford Group Movement, are struck by it. One such observer, Ellen Herman, notes: "The [12-Step] programs' core concept...is

decidedly apolitical. . . In particular, the programs' philosophy
. . . emphasizes the person and problem in isolation from any outside
social forces."[3]

Another ideological correspondence between A.A. and the Oxford
Groups can be found in their attitude toward recruitment of those
who have (had) doubts about their programs. The Oxford Groups
encouraged doubters, including agnostics, to pray and to practice
"quiet times" acting "as if" they believed in God. The assumption was
that God would make himself known to the supplicator, God having
a "plan" for every human life and being ready to reveal it to anyone
who would "listen." In A.A., the approach to doubters and the
assumptions underlying that approach are identical to those of the
Oxford Groups. A.A. even has a prescriptive aphorism for newcomers harboring doubts: "Fake it until you make it." In the "Big
Book," Bill Wilson devotes an entire chapter, "We Agnostics," to this
idea. In it, he comments: "We [atheists and agnostics] found that as
soon as we were able to lay aside prejudice [that is, rational thought]
and express even a willingness to believe in a Power greater than
ourselves, we commenced to get results. . ."[4]

The concept of God implied in this belief is less than subtle. The
A.A./Oxford Group Movement conception of a deity has little to do
with Einstein's impersonal God who doesn't play dice with the universe, while it has much to do with — and is in fact indistinguishable
from — the Old Testament concept of a God who is jealously concerned with the most picayune aspects of his followers' lives.

A related similarity is that even though the roots of both A.A. and
the Oxford Groups are in evangelical Protestantism, A.A. is, and the
Oxford Group Movement was, nonsectarian. Frank Buchman and
his followers always insisted that they were not a religious
organization and were in fact a "movement" which intended to
revitalize existing religious organizations. A.A., like the Oxford
Groups, has no ties to any particular religious bodies; but it goes one
step further than the Oxford Groups and argues, not very convin-
cingly, that its program is "spiritual" rather than "religious."

An additional ideological similarity between the Oxford Groups
and A.A. is a distinct hostility to formal organization. In the Oxford
Groups this stemmed from a belief in ever-present divine guidance
which would render formal organization unnecessary. (The primary
purposes of organization are coordination and communication, and
who or what could fulfill those functions better than an all-powerful
God making his will known to all those willing to "listen"?) A.A.
inherited this hostility to formal organization and, ironically, spelled

it out in the 12 Traditions, A.A.'s organizational principles. The ninth Tradition states, in part, that "A.A., as such, ought never be organized." The results of this hostility to organization were, however, vastly different in A.A. and the Oxford Groups. A.A., thanks largely to Bill Wilson, developed an organizational structure which is completely noncoercive and very democratic, and is in fact quite similar to organizational models developed by anarchist theorists. The Oxford Group Movement, on the other hand, was always a prime example of what has been called the "tyranny of structurelessness"; it was always under the informal but dictatorial control of its founder, Frank Buchman, and remained so until his death—thanks in part, in all probability, to the fact that there was no organizational structure through which disaffected members could challenge him.

A further point of similarity between the Oxford Group Movement and A.A., and one which reflects favorably on both, is their emphasis on human equality. Unfortunately, this emphasis is based in the shared belief that human beings are equally powerless without God's guidance; but the fact remains that there was no institutionalized racism or sexism in the Oxford Group Movement, and there is none in A.A. While it's certainly true that the Oxford Groups had no real understanding of racism and did nothing effective to combat it (and were blissfully unaware of sexism), it's also true that they did in theory oppose racism; and while A.A. was hardly a leader in the fight for desegregation, it's also true that A.A. has always made real efforts to make its program available to all alcoholics regardless of their race, sex, or sexual orientation. This is not to say that many A.A. members, especially in "the sticks," are not racist, sexist, and homophobic—many are. But A.A. has always officially frowned on such prejudice.

A final, and very important, point of ideological correspondence between A.A. and the Oxford Groups is their anti-intellectualism. Given the religious basis of both organizations, this isn't surprising. Both A.A. and the Oxford Groups were based upon belief in a God who would make "His" plans known to anyone who would "listen." This belief leads directly to anti-intellectualism in that, first of all, there is no evidence that God exists, and thus a questioning intellectual approach is a direct threat to belief in God. In the second place, even if you grant that God does exist, how can you be sure that any "guidance" you receive is from God rather than your own imagination? A related question is how do you reconcile conflicting "guidance" received by different persons unless some "guidance" doesn't come from God? And if that's the case, how do you tell which "guidance" is genuine? Obviously there is no satisfactory answer to these questions, so once again an intellectual approach to these problems becomes a real threat to belief. Thus, Oxford Group members were told, "Doubt stifles and makes abortive our attempt to act upon God's guidance," and A.A. newcomers are often told, "Your best thinking got you here."

A related stylistic similarity between A.A. and the Oxford Groups is an emphasis upon emotional experience. This stems from their common evangelical roots. Oxford Group Movement meetings were openly evangelical and often very emotional, and a great many observers have commented upon the revival-like quality of Alcoholics Anonymous meetings with their prayers, confessions, collections, rituals and witnessing.

A rather odd correspondence between A.A. and the Oxford Groups is the extensive use of slogans, aphorisms, and folk sayings. Some MRA slogans sound downright bizarre to the modern ear: "P-R-A-Y: Powerful Radiograms Always Yours," "A spiritual radiophone in every home," "Crows are black the world over," "When man listens, God speaks," "World-changing through life changing," "Minute Men of God," and "J-E-S-U-S: Just Exactly Suits Us Sinners." In A.A., one frequently hears "One Day at a Time," "Easy Does It," "Let Go and Let God," "Keep It Simple" (sometimes "Keep It Simple Stupid," KISS), "Utilize, Don't Analyze," "Fake It Until You Make It," "One Drink, One Drunk," and a number of similar homely homilies.

A harmless, and indeed attractive, stylistic feature of both A.A. and the Oxford Groups is informality. Until late in his life, his followers usually referred to Frank Buchman simply as "Frank," and by all accounts Oxford Group Movement houseparties were extremely informal affairs with attendees coming and going as they pleased, addressing each other by first names, and spending much time on leisure activities. A.A. is similarly informal. First names are habitually used at A.A. meetings, service workers at A.A. offices are almost invariably friendly and helpful, and members often engage in informal socializing, such as going out for coffee, after meetings. Given the terrible problem of loneliness in American society, it would be surprising indeed if many alcoholics didn't find the friendliness and informality of A.A. to be its most attractive features.

A not-so-attractive stylistic similarity between the two organizations is self-preoccupation. Again, this stems directly from their shared belief in divine guidance. Frank Buchman and his followers believed that their movement was directly controlled by God and was *the* answer to all human problems. Therefore, all attempts at social improvement outside of the Oxford Groups' sphere were dead ends as well as distractions from the *only* essential work, that of the Oxford Groups. A.A. isn't as grandiose in its claims as the Oxford Groups, but probably a large majority of A.A. members would vocally affirm that A.A. is the *only* route to lasting sobriety, and one often hears comments at meetings to the effect that "A.A. always works" for those who honestly try it. Since A.A. "always works" (except for those who lack "honesty" or have other "defects of character"), there is no need to develop alternative treatments, and attempts to develop and implement such alternatives are useless at best and could be harmful in that they might lead alcoholics away from the *only* effective treatment for alcoholism, A.A. The blindness and arrogance such irrational beliefs engender are so obvious as to need no further comment.

One initial similarity between A.A. and the Oxford Groups disappeared decades ago. The Oxford Group Movement was always aimed primarily at the influential and well to do, just as A.A. originally was. That A.A. initially attracted upper class and upper middle class alcoholics isn't terribly surprising given the fact that A.A.'s founders were a Wall Street insider and a surgeon, both of whom came from privileged backgrounds, and were, to boot, both members of the Oxford Group Movement before they met.

Within a relatively few years of A.A.'s inception, however, A.A.'s composition had changed dramatically, probably due to A.A.'s emphasis upon a desire to give up drinking being the sole requirement for membership. This is in stark contrast to the Buchmanites' emphasis upon recruiting "up-and-outers" and "key men." At present, A.A. membership cuts across all class lines, though it does seem to be drawn primarily from the middle class.

One dissimilarity between the two groups reflects very well upon A.A. — the question of anonymity. The Oxford Group Movement went to great lengths to attract the wealthy and prominent and, once they were hooked, assiduously used their names in its self-promotions. In addition, the Oxford Groups routinely went to great lengths to obtain endorsements, or statements which could be misrepresented as endorsements, from presidents, prime ministers, tycoons, and sports and show business figures. The Oxford Group Movement also built a veritable cult of personality around its founder, Frank Buchman, and Buchman himself left no stone unturned in his efforts to inflate his own reputation.

In contrast, A.A. insists that members maintain strict anonymity in relations with the media, and that principles must be placed before personalities—behaviors which the emphasis on anonymity helps to ensure. It is true that Bill Wilson was venerated within A.A. while he was alive, but it's also true that Wilson did his best to keep out of the public limelight and, among other things, refused to accept six honorary degrees, including an honorary Doctor of Law degree from Yale. In regard to the questions of anonymity and acting from principles rather than desire for personal aggrandizement, A.A.'s behavior, in contrast to that of the Oxford Groups, could hardly be more exemplary.

These are only the most outstanding similarities and differences between Alcoholics Anonymous and the Oxford Group Movement. Anyone thoroughly familiar with A.A. and the Oxford Groups should be able to discover other points of correspondence and divergence.

---

1. See, for example, "The Oxford Group Movement," by Henry P. Van Dusen in *The Atlantic Monthly*, August 1934, p. 249; and *Saints Run Mad*, by Marjorie Harrison. London: John Lane The Bodley Head, 1934, pp. 27-29.
2. Quoted in "The Oxford Group—Genuine or a Mockery?," *Literary Digest*, January 28, 1933, p. 17.
3. "The Twelve-Step program: Cure or cover," in *The Utne Reader,* Nov./Dec. 1988, p. 61.
4. *Alcoholics Anonymous*, by Bill Wilson. New York: Alcoholics Anonymous World Services, 1985, p. 46.

5

The 12 Steps

[This chapter draws upon "Divine Intervention and the Treatment of Chemical Dependency," the paper by Drs. Albert Ellis and Eugene Schoenfeld mentioned in Dr. Ellis's introduction, and *The Case Against Religiosity*, by Dr. Ellis. Any insights contained in this chapter are very probably the responsibility of the good doctors; any inaccuracies are my responsibility alone. — C.B.]

The 12 Steps are the backbone of the A.A. "program." A majority of Alcoholics Anonymous members regard them in the same reverent manner fundamentalist Christians regard the 10 Commandments. It's unlikely that this is an accident considering the overtly religious nature of the Steps. The 12 Steps were drawn directly from the teachings of the Oxford Groups, the evangelical Christian movement to which Bill Wilson and Dr. Bob Smith belonged and in which A.A. (though not under the A.A. name) functioned until the late 1930s.

Bill Wilson makes the connection between the Oxford Groups and the A.A. "program" crystal clear in *Alcoholics Anonymous Comes of Age*, in which he directly credits the Oxford Groups as the source of the fundamentally religious teachings codified in the 12 Steps.[1] In the Oxford Groups, the concepts embodied in the Steps were prescribed as the cure for *sin*. In A.A., these same principles are prescribed as the cure for *alcoholism*. Thus, *religion* is presented as the cure for what is commonly considered a *disease*.

Unfortunately, the hold of A.A. upon the field of alcoholism treatment is so tight that this obvious fact is almost never mentioned in either the popular press or professional journals. When this fact is (rarely) pointed out in the mass media, more often than not it's "balanced" by the disingenuous claim that A.A.'s program is "spiritual" rather than "religious."

A great many members of A.A., probably a large majority, regard the Steps as fundamental to their own recovery, and often vocally maintain that recovery is *impossible* without following the Steps. Is this true? Are the 12 Steps essential to recovery, and are alcoholics who reject them doomed to an early death from alcoholism? Fortunately, the answer is "no" to both parts of the question. If it were "yes," the many thousands of members of Secular Organizations for Sobriety, Rational Recovery, Women for Sobriety, and Men for Sobriety wouldn't be sober today, nor would the multitude — probably millions — of persons who have recovered from alcohol abuse without participating in *any* recovery program.

Why then do so many members of Alcoholics Anonymous zealously promote the 12 Steps, and why — in the face of convincing contradictory evidence — do they maintain that the Steps are essential to recovery? The answer can only be that their position is the result of religious belief, not the result of logical thinking.

Fully half of the 12 Steps explicitly mention "God," "a Power greater than ourselves," or "Him." Most religious A.A. members have little or no problem with this terminology. It fits their belief system. And just as they have no problem believing, in the absence of evidence, that God exists, they have no problem insisting, in the presence of contradictory evidence, that the 12 Steps are essential to recovery.

But what of formerly non-religious alcoholics who embrace the 12 Steps? Virtually without exception they "got religion" when they were in desperate straits. They underwent religious conversion.

Normally, happy, well-adjusted persons do not radically change their views; and, especially, they do not normally adopt views which they regard as silly and irrational. On the other hand, when a person is in an emotional crisis, radical alteration in beliefs, including religious conversion, is not unusual. As Drs. Ellis and Schoenfeld point out, "A person may be so desperate and beaten that his or her normal beliefs can be temporarily suspended, as in 'there are no atheists in foxholes'. Yes, the drowning may grasp at any straw."[2] In probably 999 cases out of 1000, then, the acceptance of the 12 Steps by formerly non-religious alcoholics is no more based in rationality and respect for facts than is the acceptance of the 12 Steps by religious alcoholics.

Another likely reason why many members of A.A. tightly embrace the 12 Steps is that the Steps provide structure, a well groomed path to follow, in shattered lives. That can look awfully attractive when your world has turned upside down and you no longer have your best friend — alcohol — to lean on. It seems probable that to a great extent the substance of the Steps is irrelevant; what is seemingly more important is simply that the Steps are there and that those dependent on them believe that they're the means of overcoming alcoholism. Another way of spelling recovery-via-the-Steps could very well be p-l-a-c-e-b-o e-f-f-e-c-t. That would largely explain why those who believe in the Steps cling to them so stubbornly.

Nevertheless, in the end it is their religious content which leads to blind adherence to the Steps. Life is filled with annoyances, dangers, and uncertainties, and, like most people, A.A. true believers don't want to face such unpleasant things. They want a "Higher Power" to take care of their problems; and, since there is no evidence that their heavenly Big Brother exists, they desperately cling to the *belief* that it does. As Albert Ellis notes, "This is like a young boy's believing that he must have a kindly father in order to survive; and then, when his father is unkind, or perhaps has died, the boy dreams up a father . . . and insists that this dream-father actually exists."[3]

In itself, this is a sad state of affairs. What makes it truly worrisome is that many, probably most, members of Alcoholics Anonymous not only embrace the irrational belief in a "Higher Power" and all of the other guilt-ridden, moralistic concepts in the 12 Steps, but they actively promote the idea that their irrational belief system is the *only* road to sobriety. I believe that they do this primarily for self-validation; they want to assure themselves that they're doing the right thing. This attempt at self-validation with its fixation on the A.A. program often leads to lack of concern for those who have alcohol problems but do not want to participate in A.A. In fact, from what I've observed, at least a few members of A.A. enjoy seeing nonreligious alcoholics drink themselves to death. It provides confirmation of their "spiritual" beliefs.

Unfortunately, many non-religious alcoholics *do* drink themselves to death after investigating A.A. and rejecting it because of its religiosity. In all too many cases that appears to be the result of their acceptance of the A.A. myth that alcoholics who reject A.A. are doomed to an alcoholic hell. This belief frequently becomes a self-fulfilling prophecy. If those too honest to "fake it until [they] make it" believe that their only choice is between abandoning their integrity (by embracing A.A.'s religious program) and participating in an endless series of dreary meetings or continuing to drink, it's little wonder that a great many eventually do drink themselves to death.

But what of the 12 Steps themselves? Are they the magic key to sobriety? A formula for mental enslavement? Or are they a combination of good, useful principles and unhealthy, pernicious dogma? The best way to answer the question is to consider the Steps individually:

1. We admitted we were powerless over alcohol. . . that our lives had become unmanageable.

This, like all of the other Steps, stems directly from Oxford Group Movement/Moral Re-Armament beliefs. A central tenet of Oxford Group Movement dogma is that the vast majority of "men" (the terminology is their responsibility) are "defeated" and are powerless in themselves to overcome their "defeat." The original version of the first Step shows its lineage very clearly: "1. We admitted that we were licked, that we were powerless over alcohol."[4]

This is not to say that Step 1 is all bad. A very important and useful principle — the overcoming of denial — is contained in the first Step. Until a person admits that s/he has a problem, s/he will almost certainly do nothing about it.

At the same time, the first Step stresses personal *powerlessness*. It's difficult to see how this can do anything for those who accept this Step other than contribute to low self-esteem. This is pernicious in that if there's one common denominator among those who do harmful things to themselves, such as drinking excessively, it's that they have a low opinion of themselves.

In fact there is evidence that A.A.'s emphasis upon individual powerlessness over alcohol consumption — where taking a single drink is regarded as a catastrophe — significantly contributes to worsen relapses. In the March-April 1987 issue of the professional journal *Social Work*, Dennis Daley states:

> "Teaching clients to expect one episode of use to lead to total loss of control may set the expectation that initial use cannot be curtailed before a full-blown relapse occurs. . . In the course of treating hundreds of relapsed substance abusers, my colleagues and I found that our clients reported that they thought total loss of control was inevitable or that the initial substance use behavior meant that they could not recover."[5]

Daley does go on to state, however, that many alcoholics who experience a "slip" without its turning into a serious relapse become overconfident, continue to drink, and eventually do have full-blown relapses. This, paradoxical though it may seem, is quite likely a result of the A.A. myth that picking up the first drink inevitably and quickly leads to renewed alcoholic drinking. It's an example of what could be termed the "boy who cried wolf effect." After discovering that the dire warnings about the immediate and disastrous consequences of the "first drink" are not based in fact, it would be little wonder if many alcoholics didn't conclude that *all* warnings against renewed drinking are similarly incorrect, and would then go on to a gradually worsening pattern of excessive drinking. In fact, judging from Daley's data, this is exactly what happens in many cases. It would be a healthy development if A.A. would abandon its unrealistic emphasis on loss of control after the first drink, and would instead preach that picking up the first drink is a mistake, though not necessarily a catastrophic one, and that continuing to drink after that first "slip" is playing with fire.

In sum, the first Step embodies one healthy, useful principle (the overcoming of denial) and one pernicious, harmful principle (personal powerlessness, especially as related to drinking behavior).

2. Came to believe that a Power greater than ourselves could restore us to sanity.

Again, this stems directly from Oxford Group Movement teachings. Oxford Groupers fervently believed that the individual was powerless and that there was an all-powerful God who could, and would, resolve *all* human problems if "men" would only turn their lives over to "Him." Of course, this belief implies the existence of a God which can only be described as crudely anthropomorphic— a God vitally concerned with human problems, including the most trivial. It's difficult to see the results of such a belief as anything other than atrocious.

Step 2 is doubly pernicious. Its very religiosity is a major problem for many persons. Like Steps 3, 5, 6, 7 and 11 it refers to "God," "Him," or "a Power greater than ourselves." (Note the capitalization.) This poses obvious problems for those who believe that the existence of God is no more likely than the existence of Mother Goose. It's little wonder that a great many atheists and agnostics reject A.A. and its Steps rather than renounce their honest beliefs.

When A.A. newcomers express doubts about the religiosity of the second Step, they're normally told that their "Higher Power" can be anything they choose. Doorknobs, bedpans, and A.A. itself are often suggested as "Higher Powers" for atheist and agnostic newcomers. It doesn't seem to bother those making such suggestions that the very next Step explicitly mentions "God."

Even for religious persons, the second Step is harmful in that, like the first Step, it promotes the idea of individual helplessness. It encourages A.A. members to be dependent. This is directly contrary to the normal therapeutic goal of helping individuals to become independent and self-directed.

3. Made a decision to turn our will and our lives over to the care of God *as we understood Him.*

This Step poses obvious problems for atheist and agnostic newcomers who have chosen, for example, a doorknob as their "Power greater than [themselves]." How does one turn one's life over to a doorknob?

Again, this Step was lifted directly from the Oxford Groups dogma mentioned in the discussion of Step 2. Indeed, the central tenet of the Oxford Groups was that God would reveal "Himself" to anyone who would "listen," and that "He" had a minutely detailed plan for every human life. The sheer *chutzpah* of this belief is positively breathtaking. It's the most grandiose excuse imaginable for the evasion of individual thought, responsibility, and decision making.

A particularly harmful aspect of this Step is that it demands dependence on a "God" whose existence has never been demonstrated. If someone truly believed that "God" was keeping him or her from drinking and — perhaps because of the death of a loved one or some other traumatic event — was shocked into the realization this his or her "God" very probably didn't exist, s/he could well begin to drink again.

As Drs. Ellis and Schoenfeld point out, *anything* encouraging individual effort and responsibility — even the religious saying, "God helps those who help themselves" — would be preferable to this Step.

4. Made a searching and fearless moral inventory of ourselves.

This could be a very useful principle — and not just for alcoholics. A searching and fearless self-examination is obviously useful to those attempting to rebuild shattered lives, as recovering alcoholics are (or to those simply attempting to live happier, more productive lives). Few things are more useful to recovering alcoholics than discovering the reasons *why* they drank excessively. For once they've discovered those reasons, especially the irrational beliefs which made drinking seem attractive, they can deal with them.

Unfortunately, the fourth Step doesn't call for an inventory of irrational beliefs, physical causes, or other contributory factors; it calls for a *moral* inventory. What this has to do with recovery from alcoholism is anybody's guess. Unless one believes that alcoholism is caused by *sin*, this Step makes no sense whatsoever.

Unfortunately, Bill Wilson was an enthusiastic Oxford Grouper and *did*, at bottom, believe that alcoholism was caused by sin. If Wilson actually believed that alcoholism was caused by an "allergy," as Dr. Silkworth speculates in the "Big Book,"[6] it's extremely difficult to see why he would have included the guilt-inducing term "moral" in this Step. But at the time he wrote the Steps, Wilson regarded the Oxford Group Movement as his rescuer, and so it was natural that he would share the assumption of the Groups that all human problems are a direct result of sin.

The only purpose the fourth Step can serve is to produce guilt, and hence low self-esteem. Again, this seems more likely to contribute to self-damaging rather than self-caring behavior.

5. Admitted to God, to ourselves, and to another human being the exact nature of our wrongs.

This is still another legacy of the Oxford Groups. "Confession" was an integral part of the Oxford Group program, and Group Movement founder, Frank Buchman, was an expert at extracting confessions (often of a sexual nature) from potential converts. Confession of sin was considered so important by Buchman that he included it as one of the "5 Cs," which were a schematic outline of the Group program, and were reportedly utilized by conservative A.A. groups well into the 1940s: "Confidence, Conviction, Confession, Conversion, Continuance." Thus it was natural that Grouper Bill Wilson would include confession as a key element of the A.A. program. It should be noted, though, that in order to make this Step more palatable to nonreligious alcoholics, Wilson used the euphemism "our wrongs" when what he undoubtedly really meant was "our sins."

Still, a gem is buried here amidst the reference to "God" and the moralistic term "our wrongs." The buried gem is honesty and openness. Practicing alcoholics live in a state of denial—that is, unwillingness to acknowledge their condition—and normally are unwilling to honestly discuss their use of alcohol and many other subjects which hit too close to home. The willingness to openly and honestly discuss sensitive personal matters is a huge step toward recovery, self-acceptance and a happier life.

Unfortunately, the principle of honesty and openness is largely obscured by the religious and moralistic terminology of the fifth Step. The use of the term "our wrongs" (in other words, "our sins") is only an inducement to guilt. It seems very odd in the guiding principles of an organization which actively promotes the belief that alcoholism is a disease. If alcoholism is indeed a disease, the use of guilt-inducing moralistic terminology can only be seen as a way of blaming the victim (of disease).

The reference to "another human being" introduces us to the concept of "sponsors." Newcomers in A.A. are routinely urged to find a sponsor (a more experienced member of A.A. with whom they develop a special relationship, to whom they make a confession of their "wrongs," and from whom they receive guidance and indoctrination) shortly after they enter "the program." Sponsors, of course, vary greatly. Some genuinely try to be helpful, while others are meddlesome busybodies who enjoy controlling other human beings. The therapeutic value of the sponsor relationship certainly seems suspect in that it, like virtually everything else in the A.A. program, encourages dependence.

6. Were entirely ready to have God remove all these defects of character.

This is yet another Step which invokes "God" and which encourages dependency rather than independence. It's interesting to speculate how those who chose doorknobs or bedpans as their "Higher Power" work this Step. This Step is another expression of the Oxford Group belief in an all-powerful, anthropomorphic God with a detailed plan for every human life, which "He" will reveal if human beings will only "listen." Needless to say, "defects of character" is almost certainly another euphemism for "sins," and is employed to disguise the religious nature of the Steps.

7. Humbly asked Him to remove our shortcomings.

Humility is the virtue of those with poor self-images. In our cultural context, it's a purely religious, Judeo-Christian concept: Human beings are sinful wretches and should be properly humble before a perfect God who will resolve all of their problems if they properly abase themselves. Nonbelievers often find this concept revolting, and it would be surprising if this Step in and of itself didn't drive countless alcoholics away from A.A. It's interesting to note that the original version of Step 7 included the words "on our knees" after the word "humbly." In light of this Step, it seems absurd that A.A. continues to maintain that its program is "spiritual" rather than "religious."

Step 7 is yet another assertion of individual helplessness and the desirability of dependency and guilt—things which were at the heart of the Oxford Group program. In the Oxford Groups (after "Confidence" in the "soul surgeon" was established) guilt was considered a desirable and necessary precursor to "Conviction, Confession, Conversion, Continuance."

8. Made a list of persons we had harmed, and became willing to make amends to such people wherever possible.

This Step stems directly from the personal experience of Oxford Group Movement founder Frank Buchman, specifically from his much ballyhooed writing of apologetic letters after his "conversion" at Keswick in 1908. After writing the letters, Buchman reportedly felt a great sense of release, and henceforth regarded making amends as an essential aspect of his spiritual program.

Making a list of those one has harmed is a useful practice in so far as it goes, and is an important tool in coming to a full realization of the effects one's alcoholism had on other human beings. But this Step begs the question of whether those we've harmed *want* to hear from us again. In a great many cases they're probably happy to have forgotten us, or at least to have gotten us out of their lives, and re-contacting them could easily reopen old wounds.

The eighth Step (and indeed the entire A.A. program), with its emphasis on individual culpability and total disregard of social factors, bears more than a passing resemblance to "new age" sophistry which insists that we are all totally responsible for everything that happens to us. New ageism and A.A.'s eighth Step both ignore the fact that most people (including alcoholics) are the victims of far more wrongs than they commit. We're all the victims of government and corporate intrusions into our personal lives and finances; the vast majority of us are economically exploited and ripped off; we're all victims of environmental despoliation for private profit; and huge numbers of us are the victims of racism, sexism and homophobia.

But you won't find a hint of this in A.A.'s program. For example, it's a well-established fact that the level of alcohol abuse rises (as do the rates of child abuse and wife beating) when unemployment levels rise. Alcoholics Anonymous, however, totally ignores this and all other social factors which contribute to alcoholism. Instead, A.A. lays the entire blame for alcoholism on the shoulders of alcoholics with its references to "our wrongs," "our shortcomings" and making "amends."

Making a list of those we have harmed is a useful exercise. It would be at least as useful if we'd also make a list of those who have harmed us, especially the social institutions responsible, in most cases, for the bulk of the harm. This would be a more holistic approach and would provide a more complete picture of the conditions in which we became active alcoholics.

9. Made direct amends to such people wherever possible, except when to do so would injure them or others.

This is a useful thing to do. It deepens the understanding of what effects our actions had on others when we were active alcoholics, and of the risks we'd run if we would start to drink again. In addition, it gives a sense of closure to an unhappy period in our lives. But, again, the question of whether those we've injured *want* to hear from us is ignored.

It would be healthier, however, to also begin to work to change the social conditions which contributed to our becoming alcoholics. This could, conceivably, lead to direct social improvements; and at the very least it would enhance personal empowerment. Active engagement, rather than passive acceptance, increases self-esteem.

10. Continued to take personal inventory and when we were wrong promptly admitted it.

This is essentially a restatement of Step 4. It's also an expression of the Oxford Group principle of "Continuance." Unfortunately, Step 10 doesn't state what *kind* of personal inventory we should continue to take. Since the only type mentioned earlier in the Steps was a *moral* inventory, one can only conclude that continuing to take such an "inventory" will lead to more guilt, low self-esteem, and groveling "humbly" before the "Power" which "restore[s]" A.A. members to "sanity." The tenth Step also implies that there is no escape from the A.A. program—if you accept it, you'll be participating in it for the rest of your life.

11. Sought through prayer and meditation to improve our conscious contact with God *as we understood Him*, praying only for knowledge of His will for us and the power to carry that out.

This is still another tiresome call to dependency, other-directedness, and disregard for facts, logic and rationality. Not incidentally, seeking such "guidance" from God was considered the *only* legitimate reason for prayer by the Oxford Groups. This Step is an expression of the Oxford Group belief in "two-way" prayer in which God both listens and makes his wishes known. In view of this Step, with its repeated calls for *prayers* to "God," the claim that A.A.'s program is "spiritual" rather than "religious" sounds downright ludicrous and more than a little dishonest.

12. Having had a spiritual awakening as the result of these Steps, we tried to carry this message to alcoholics and to practice these principles in all our affairs.

This is another expression of the Oxford Group principle of "Continuance." It was an article of faith among Groupers that once they had been "changed," they should carry the "message" to those who were still "defeated" so that they too could "change." The reference to "practic[ing] these principles in all our affairs" is an obvious echo of the Oxford Group belief that theirs was not an organization but "a way of life," as well as a foreshadowing of the subsequent A.A. claim that it too is a "way of life."

Despite its origin, there is a valuable principle embedded in this Step. Experience has shown that aiding others to become sober is very helpful to recovering alcoholics. It makes them feel useful, which builds self-esteem; and it provides a reminder of the horrifying nature of active alcoholism, which is a powerful spur to staying sober.

At the same time, Step 12 clearly indicates that A.A.'s program is a program for *life* — no one ever graduates from it. It's also indicative of A.A.'s self-absorption. Members of A.A. are not urged to help others overcome alcoholism regardless of their belief or disbelief in A.A.'s program. Rather — because A.A. has *the* answer — they are urged to "carry this [A.A.] message to alcoholics," and if those alcoholics don't want to hear the message, screw 'em.

These are A.A.'s revered 12 Steps, a combination of good, helpful principles and unhealthy, pernicious dogma. Virtually anyone with any real knowledge of alcoholism should be able to construct a sturdier set of steps to recovery.

---

1. *Alcoholics Anonymous Comes of Age*, by Bill Wilson. New York: Alcoholics Anonymous World Services, 1989, pp. 58-63, 160-167.
2. "Divine Intervention and the Treatment of Chemical Dependency," by Drs. Albert Ellis and Eugene Schoenfeld. *Journal of Substance Abuse*, No. 2, 1990, p. 463.
3. *The Case Against Religiosity*, by Dr. Albert Ellis. New York: Institute for Rational Emotive Therapy, 1983, p. 3.
4. Wilson, op. cit., p. 160.
5. "Relapse Prevention with Substance Abusers: Clinical Issues and Myths," by Dennis Daley. *Social Work*, March-April 1987, p. 140.
6. *Alcoholics Anonymous*, by Bill Wilson. New York: Alcoholics Anonymous World Services, 1976, p. xxvi.

6

The 12 Traditions

Just as the 12 Steps are a set of guiding principles for individual A.A. members, the 12 Traditions are a set of guiding principles for A.A. as an organization. The Traditions were written by Bill Wilson and are a codification of principles developed and practiced during A.A.'s early, turbulent years. The Traditions were first published in May 1946 in their "long form" in A.A.'s official organ, *The Grapevine*, and were unanimously ratified in Cleveland at the first international A.A. convention in 1950.

To a great extent the 12 Traditions explain why A.A. has survived and prospered for over half a century: they're a blueprint for organization according to noncoercive, anarchist principles. It's a tribute to the soundness and wide applicability of these principles that they were adopted as a result of the real-life experiences and problems of the A.A. fellowship—large numbers of people who, in the vast majority of cases, almost certainly knew nothing of organizational theory. As well, it's a tribute to the wide applicability of these tenets that they were codified by Bill Wilson, a life-long conservative Republican. (While a discussion of anarchist organizational principles might seem out of place in an analysis of A.A., it's inescapable in that A.A. is organized strictly in accord with those principles. Since most readers will probably have little interest in this topic, though, discussion will be kept to the minimum necessary.)

While the 12 Traditions are overall much sounder and more humane that the 12 Steps, the Traditions, like the Steps, are a mixed bag of sound, useful concepts and worse-than-useless religiosity. (The comments on religiosity will be perfunctory in this chapter because extensive treatment would essentially duplicate criticisms of religiosity in the previous chapter and in Appendix C.)

The following discussion will use the "short form" of the Traditions. Those interested in seeing the "long form" should consult *12 Steps and 12 Traditions*.

1. Our common welfare should come first; personal recovery depends upon A.A. unity.

But for some of the other Traditions, the first Tradition could be very dangerous. The idea that the individual is less important than the "common welfare" is, of course, the justification for invasive, coercive government and all manner of horrifying violations of individual rights. Traditions 2, 4, and 9, however, make it crystal clear that A.A. is organized on a nongovernmental (that is, noncoercive) basis. So, instead of being a call to coercion, the first Tradition is a call to cooperation.

It's also a restatement of the A.A. principle that the individual is helpless in him or herself, and that recovery is possible only through the A.A. program. The undesirable effects of this belief—especially the substitution of one form of dependency for another and the induced hopelessness this belief fosters in alcoholics who want to quit but can't stand A.A. — were dealt with in the previous chapter.

2. For our group purpose there is but one ultimate authority—a loving God as He may express Himself in our group conscience. Our leaders are but trusted servants; they do not govern.

Stripped of its religious terminology, the first sentence simply means that A.A. will operate in accordance with the desires of its membership. The second sentence is equally important. The idea that officers (or "leaders") should serve rather than govern is a cornerstone of any group organized along anarchist principles, as A.A. is. In *12 Steps and 12 Traditions*, Bill Wilson wisely notes, "our group conscience, well-advised by its elders, will be in the long run wiser than any single leader."[1]

This Tradition finds expression in A.A.'s organizational form and decision-making process. To ensure that no ruling elite emerges, there are regular elections for all A.A. offices; all major decisions are made by majority vote at both local and national level; and officers have neither the power to determine who is or isn't an A.A. member, nor to control the activities of the membership.

Another safeguard against the formation of a ruling elite which other organizations organized on anarchist principles normally take, but which is only "recommend[ed]" in A.A., is the rotation of offices.[2] This does not refer to the simple holding of elections at regular intervals, but rather to prohibition against individuals serving more than one term. Though this is only a "recommend[ation]" in A.A., it seems to be vigorously adhered to in practice.

3. The only requirement for A.A. membership is a desire to stop drinking.

This is another very healthy principle. It ensures that anyone who comes to A.A. for help will not be turned away; and it goes a long way toward explaining why A.A.'s membership is so diverse. But it also means that A.A. has no formal way to rid itself of troublesome and disruptive members.

Perhaps surprisingly, this has not proven to be much of a problem. From my observations, disruptive persons rarely show up at meetings more than once, and when they do, they're generally "bad vibed" out of them. Group opinion is a very powerful force for assuring adherence to group behavioral norms. Unfortunately, it is such a powerful force that a great many persons who come to A.A. for help, but who disagree with A.A. dogma, are also "bad vibed" out of A.A. meetings.

4. Each group should be autonomous except in matters affecting other groups or A.A. as a whole.

This is the principle of decentralism. It's an additional safeguard against the emergence of a ruling elite. The only conditions A.A. places on group autonomy are, "A group ought not to do anything which would greatly injure A.A. as a whole, nor should it affiliate itself with anything or anybody else." The prohibition against injurious activities is normal in organizations of any type, though the prohibition against affiliation with other entities or individuals is not. In this particular, A.A. departs markedly from specifically anarchist groups. Most such groups are interested in a wide range of issues and normally will work with other organizations toward common goals. A.A., on the other hand, is a single-interest group which believes it has *the* answer to alcoholism and is solely concerned with the spread of its "program." A.A. does, however, maintain informal ties (through members with dual affiliations) with other organizations. In particular, the National Council on Alcohol and Other Drug Addictions, which was founded by A.A. member Marty Mann and which counted Bill Wilson and Dr. Bob Smith among its sponsors, is closely tied to A.A. and seems to function as A.A.'s lobbying arm and spokesman on controversial issues.

5. Each group has but one primary purpose—to carry its message to the alcoholic who still suffers.

There's both a good side and a bad side to this Tradition. The good side is that having a single focus promotes group cohesiveness—

there's no wrangling about organizational direction—and that this particular focus serves a therapeutic end. Proselytizing to other alcoholics gives a sense of purpose to A.A. members and tends to increase their self-esteem by helping them feel useful.

The bad side of this Tradition is that it promotes the idea that A.A. has *the* answer to the problem of alcoholism. (Notice that the primary purpose of A.A. groups as defined in this Tradition is to "carry" the A.A. "message" to alcoholics—not to help alcoholics sober up.) The negative consequences of this—arrogance, self-absorption, hostility to non-12 Step alcoholism recovery programs, etc.—were dealt with in the previous chapter.

6. An A.A. group ought never endorse, finance, or lend the A.A. name to any related facility or outside enterprise, lest problems of money, property, and prestige divert us from our primary purpose.

This is a wise principle. Involvement with commercial enterprises would certainly alter the nature of any Alcoholics Anonymous group; it would move it away from being an all-volunteer, self-help organization. Further, given the sleazy nature of many, if not most, American businesses, association with commercial ventures could easily give A.A. a bad name.

Unfortunately, A.A. has adhered to the letter of this Tradition rather than its spirit. At this writing, involvement in A.A. groups is prescribed as part of treatment in virtually *all* hospital and institutional alcoholism treatment programs; as a consequence, approximately 50 percent of all A.A. literature sold is sold to these instutions.[3] The profits from these sales makes up a significant part of the budget for A.A.'s General Service Office. In 1988, contributions from A.A. groups were $1,045,300 less than the cost of group services; income from sales of publications to institutions covered this shortfall.[4] While A.A. is not paid directly for its services by institutional programs, they do provide A.A. with meeting space, a huge market for its literature, and a steady (and growing) pool of recruits. So, it could easily be argued that A.A. has a vested interest in maintenance of the present alcoholism treatment industry.

7. Every A.A. group ought to be fully self-supporting, declining outside contributions.

To those inundated by junk mail begging for their hard-earned dollars, A.A.'s seventh Tradition sounds strange indeed. But it embodies one of the most intelligent principles A.A. has adopted.

As Bill Wilson notes in *12 Steps and 12 Traditions*, "Whoever pays the piper is apt to call the tune."[5] One of A.A.'s prime goals is to keep control of the organization in the hands of its membership; and this vow of corporate poverty, the seventh Tradition, is an important guarantee of this. The seventh Tradition is intended to keep the organization's service structure dependent upon the membership as a whole for financial support. It's also designed to keep individual A.A. groups self-directed.

If A.A. as a whole, or individual A.A. groups, accepted large contributions, those making the contributions could easily end up having undue influence even if they didn't intend to. The way that this normally occurs is that an organization will accept one large donation from an individual, then another, and before anyone notices it, the organization has become dependent on the donor. Then, even if the donor makes no demands, the group becomes *very* careful not to do anything which could alienate the donor. Thus, even if they don't intend it, those who give large sums of money often end up with undue influence.

Unfortunately, A.A.'s dependence upon money derived from literature sales to institutions seems to subvert, at least in part, the intention of this Tradition. At present, the services provided to groups by the General Service Office cost more than the groups as a whole donate to meet G.S.O. expenses. Thus, those groups — nearly *half* — which don't contribute a dime toward G.S.O. expenses are to some extent non-self-supporting.

8. Alcoholics Anonymous should remain forever nonprofessional, but our service centers may employ special workers.

On the surface this seems remarkably similar to the policy of anarchist political groups which employ service workers, but have no "professional" staff. The reason for A.A.'s policy is, however, different in one important respect from that of anarchist groups. Anarchists avoid "professionalization" of their organizations because they wish to avoid creating hierarchies; they want to keep their organizations as democratic as possible, something which the creation of an "expert" or "professional" class would work against. To that end, when necessary, they employ service workers whose duties and responsibilities are carefully limited, and who it is clearly understood do not set policy.

This wariness of a "professional" governing class certainly seems to be a large part of the reason for the eighth Tradition, but A.A. also feels that professionalism "does not work for us."[6] Unfortunately, this insistence that professionalism—especially professional treatment independent of A.A.—does not work tends to lock A.A. into its regrettable we've-got-the-answer mindset. The positive aspect of this Tradition is that it does go a long way toward preventing the formation of a professional bureaucracy dictating policy to members.

9. A.A., as such, ought never be organized; but we may create service boards or committees directly responsible to those they serve.

This Tradition demonstrates that its author, Bill Wilson, was just as confused as most members of the public are about what does and what does not constitute organization. The discussion of organization in *12 Steps and 12 Traditions* makes it extremely clear that Wilson shared the popular misconception that organization is synonymous with coercive, hierarchical organization. The clearest expression of this belief is his statement: "Power to direct or govern is the essence of organization everywhere."[7]

This assertion, which assumes that hierarchy and coercion are essential to organization, is demonstrably false. Organization, according to a dictionary definition, is merely "the state or manner of being organized...into a whole consisting of interdependent or coordinated parts, especially for harmonious or united action." Another way of stating this is that organization is a form of systematization for the purposes of communication and coordinated action. Thus, the questions of coercion and hierarchy are external to the question of organization. Coercive, hierarchical organizations, such as government and large corporations, exemplify but one type of organization.

A brief glance at present-day society reveals thousands of organizations which do not employ coercion. Some examples of organizations based on voluntary cooperation are the Red Cross, the National Organization for Women, the U.S. Chess Federation, Mensa, the American Radio Relay League (the national ham radio organization), and innumerable food co-ops and other mutual aid groups. Some of these are nonhierarchical in addition to being noncoercive. As well, a glance at history reveals nonhierarchical mass labor organizations, such as the IWW in the U.S. and the Confederación Nacional del Trabajo in Spain, based purely on voluntary cooperation.[8]

But perhaps the most telling argument against the idea that

coercion and hierarchy are necessary to organization is A.A. itself. A.A. is probably the best current example of a mass organization organized along anarchist (i.e., noncoercive) lines. It's a tribute to the efficacy of the noncoercive principle of organization that it functions so well in an organization composed overwhelmingly of persons totally ignorant of anarchist theory and history, and almost certainly violently opposed to anarchism (or what they mistakenly suppose it to be) as a political philosophy.[9]

It's more than a bit ironic that the creation of "service boards or committees directly responsible to those they serve" is a cornerstone of the type of organization Bill Wilson didn't recognize — noncoercive organization.

10. Alcoholics Anonymous has no opinion on outside issues; hence the A.A. name ought never be drawn into public controversy.

This is undoubtedly a wise guiding principle for a single-interest group. It allows members with widely divergent views on other topics to work together effectively in pursuit of their one common interest. For an organization such as a chess club, it makes a lot of sense. Whether this principle also makes sense for an organization dealing with a social problem is open to question.

A.A. adopted this Tradition largely because of the experience of the Washingtonian Society in the 1840s and 1850s. Like A.A., the Washingtonians were originally a self-help organization of alcoholics rooted in Protestant evangelicalism. They had considerable success; the society had more than 100,000 members at its high point. But the Washingtonians expanded their activities to embrace other reform causes such as abolitionism and the temperance movement. They were soon mired in internal and external controversy and disappeared within a few years. (It seems relevant to point out that had they confined themselves to social issues directly contributing to alcoholism — or had they kept officially aloof, but encouraged members to form voluntary special interest groups to work on such social issues — the outcome of their story might have been different.)

Unfortunately, the tenth Tradition is also an expression of the A.A. belief that alcoholism is purely an individual problem unrelated to political, social, and economic conditions. If A.A. were to adopt the more realistic view that alcoholism has socioeconomic contributory factors, it would be very difficult for A.A. to avoid "public controversy"— especially if it wanted to actively work to mitigate the

socio-economic factors which help to produce alcoholism. Even if
A.A. *didn't* want to deal directly with the social, economic and
political factors which contribute to alcoholism, it would still be a
huge advance if A.A. would simply admit that these factors exist.

Instead, A.A. continues to lay total responsibility for alcoholism
directly on the shoulders of alcoholics—a position inherently supportive of the socioeconomic status quo. If alcoholism is completely
the responsibility of individuals, by definition it has no causes (or
contributory factors) in the social realm; and hence there is no need
whatsoever for changes in the social structure in order to eliminate,
or reduce the level of, alcoholism—all that's necessary is that
individual alcoholics adopt the A.A. program.

11. Our public relations policy is based on attraction rather than
promotion; we need always maintain personal anonymity at the level
of press, radio, and films.

This two-part policy has served A.A. well. The deliberate policy of
avoiding organizational self-promotion has resulted in a tremendous
amount of favorable publicity for A.A. in the mass media. The
attraction-not-promotion approach has worked well for two reasons:
1) A.A. is well intentioned and is widely believed to be doing great
good in alleviating a serious social problem; 2) A.A., with its religious orientation, emphasis on individual responsibility and solutions, and disregard of the social factors involved in alcoholism, fits
snugly into the existing social order. So, it should be no surprise that
the corporate-controlled media treat A.A. in a friendly manner. It's
doubtful that A.A.'s non-self-promoting policy would work as well
for a more controversial organization. (It should be noted, though,
that A.A. does employ televised public service announcements
advertising its services; this seems difficult to reconcile with this
Tradition.)

The second part of this policy, maintaining personal anonymity, is
very wise. It's still another safeguard against any individual(s)
gaining undue influence over A.A. — it's a leveling device. It's also a
safeguard against individuals using A.A. as a means of self-
promotion. Finally, it's a means by which A.A. avoids organizational
embarrassment in the event that a prominent member should resume
drinking. The policy of anonymity would serve many other organizations as well as it does A.A., and it's a pity that it isn't more widely
followed.

12. Anonymity is the spiritual foundation of all our Traditions, ever reminding us to place principles before personalities.

This is basically a restatement of the latter part of the eleventh Tradition, perhaps added for emphasis. It is refreshing, though, to see this call to act from principles rather than from a desire for self-aggrandizement. One can only wish that this principle was far more widely practiced in all spheres of social life—both inside and outside of A.A.

---

1. *12 Steps & 12 Traditions*, by Bill Wilson. New York: Alcoholics Anonymous World Services, 1982, p. 135.

2. *The A.A. Service Manual, combined with Twelve Concepts for World Service.* New York: Alcoholics Anonymous World Services, 1989, p. S72. This is another example of one of A.A.'s most attractive traits—its aversion to laying down "the law," and instead making "suggestions" and "recommendations."

3. *The A.A. Story*, by Ernest Kurtz. San Francisco: Harper & Row, 1988, p. 180

4. *Service Manual*, op. cit., p. 74.

5. *12 Steps & 12 Traditions*, op. cit., p. 164.

6. Ibid., p. 166.

7. Ibid., p. 172

8. See *Collectives in the Spanish Revolution*, by Gaston Leval. London: Freedom Press, 1975; *The Anarchist Collectives*, Sam Dolgoff, editor. New York: Free Life Editions, 1974; and *Homage to Catalonia*, by George Orwell. London: Penguin Books.

9. For expositions of anarchist organizational theory see *Anarchy in Action*, by Colin Ward. London: Freedom Press, 1973; *Fields, Factories and Workshops Tomorrow*, by Peter Kropotkin. London: Freedom Press; *About Anarchism*, by Nicolas Walter. London: Freedom Press; *Anarchism and Anarcho-Syndicalism*, by Rudolf Rocker. London: Freedom Press, 1988; *Anarcho-Syndicalism*, by Rudolf Rocker. London: Phoenix Press; and *The ABC of Anarchism*, by Alexander Berkman. London: Freedom Press.

7

Is A.A. a Cult?
(preliminary considerations)

Alcoholics Anonymous is clearly a religious organization, but is A.A. a cult? Before answering that question it's first necessary to define the key term. That's a very difficult task; there are almost as many definitions of the word "cult" as there are experts on the subject. One thing virtually all definitions of the word have in common is that they're quite broad.

Two of the definitions given by the Random House Unabridged Dictionary are fairly typical: "a group or sect bound together by devotion to or veneration of the same thing, person, ideal, etc."; and "a group having a sacred ideology and a set of rites centering around their sacred symbols."

Such definitions — as opposed to lists of attributes — could well apply to a great number of groups, many of which most people would never consider cults. Thus, the crucial question becomes what are the *specific characteristics* which distinguish cults, especially cults which are dangerous to both their own members and to society in general? Based on research into, and direct contact with, a number of groups which are commonly considered to be cults (especially Synanon, the Church of Scientology, the Unification Church [Moonies], the Church of Jesus Christ of Latter Day Saints [the Mormons], People's Temple, and the Lyndon LaRouche organization in its various permutations [National Caucus of Labor Committees, U.S. Labor Party, etc.]),[1] I would list the following traits as being characteristic. (I should note, though, that not even the most obviously dangerous cults always possess all of the following attributes, though some do.)

1) **Religious Orientation.** Cults are usually centered around belief in a "higher power"; they often have elaborate religious rituals and emphasize prayer. Current and recent religious cults include the People's Temple, the Church of Scientology, the International

Society for Krishna Consciousness (Hare Krishnas), the Unification Church, Synanon (which, significantly, declared itself a religion while developing the most unsavory aspects of a cult), the Children of God, The Way International, Jehovah's Witnesses, and the largest and most successful of the cults, the Church of Jesus Christ of Latter Day Saints (the Mormons).

While secular cults also exist, they are not as numerous as religious cults. The most obvious example of a secular cult is the LaRouche organization, which has almost all of the characteristics of a totalitarian cult other than religious orientation. Two others which I believe could properly be classified as secular cults are the Revolutionary Communist Party and the New Alliance Party. But these are the exceptions; easily 90 percent of present-day cults are religious in nature.

2) **Irrationality.** Cults discourage skepticism and rational thought. As James and Marcia Rudin note in *Prison or Paradise: The New Religious Cults*, "The groups are anti-intellectual, placing all emphasis on intuition or emotional experience. 'Knowledge' is redefined as those ideas or experiences dispensed by the group or its leader. One can only attain knowledge by joining the group and submitting to its doctrine. One cannot question this 'knowledge.' If a follower shows signs of doubting he is made to feel that the fault lies within himself, not with the ideas. . ."[2]

It's also common for cult leaders to tell their followers that doubt is the work of the devil. The Unification Church in particular has institutionalized the practices of equating doubt with sinfulness and satanic influence, and of attempting to stamp out independent thought. Some of its most common slogans (for internal use) are "Your Mind Is Fallen," "Stamp Out Doubt," and "No More Concepts."[3] If members of cults persist in having doubts, they're accused of being under satanic influence and excommunicated or, in extreme instances, even murdered, as in Ervil LeBaron's Mormon splinter group, The Church of the Blood of the Lambs of God.[4]

3) **A Charismatic Leader.** Present in most cults, the leader can be living (Synanon, Unification Church, LaRouchites) or dead (Scientology, Mormons). In cases where the leader dies, the cult either fades away, is taken over by another charismatic leader, or, as with the Scientologists and Mormons, is taken over by a pre-existing hierarchy.

4) **A Hierarchical, Authoritarian Structure.** It should be noted, though, that relatively new cults often have little structure; but as time passes, hierarchy and bureaucracy usually arise, as is to be expected in authoritarian setups. If a hierarchy does not arise—this sometimes happens because of the charismatic leader's fear of take-over attempts—the cult will probably disintegrate upon the leader's death, unless a new charismatic leader quickly arises to take his or her place.

5) **Submission of the Individual to the "Will of God"** or to some other abstraction (such as "the dictatorship of the proletariat"). This means abandonment of individual decision making in favor of obeying the will of the abstraction as interpreted by the cult. In practice, this means obeying the orders of the charismatic leader or the hierarchy which controls the group.

One outward sign of individual submission to the charismatic leader is the infantilization of members. In many instances, the People's Temple being an example, members refer to and address the leader as "Father." In many cults the submission of the individual is so complete that the charismatic leader and/or hierarchy make all significant life decisions for the individual, up to and including choice of sex and marriage partners.

In Synanon, the control of its founder, Charles Dederich, was so complete that he forced all of the male members of his cult, save himself, to undergo vasectomies.[5] He later forced all members to switch sex partners.[6] And in the Unification Church, the hierarchy picks the marriage partners of members. In that church it's common for brides and grooms to meet for the first time at their marriage ceremony.

6) **Dogmatism.** Cults invariably have *the* truth and are highly antagonistic to those who dare question it. Given that cultists have this precious commodity, they almost always view themselves as *better* than other people, which means that nonbelievers and members of rival sects are frequently seen as less than human, if not outright tools of the devil. This attitude of superiority often manifests itself in an "ends justify the means" mentality and in the use of violence against outsiders or against heretics within the group. The most lurid recent examples of such violence have been provided by Ervil LeBaron's Lambs of God,[7] though historical examples abound.

7) **Separatism.** Cult members almost always view themselves as outsiders, as different from the rest of society. One expression of separatism is the use of specialized terms — almost all cults develop a jargon peculiar to themselves. Another, though less common, manifestation is the abandonment of "old" personal names and the taking of "new" ones. A third is the adoption of distinctive dress and/or other alterations in personal appearance. The practice of head-shaving in Synanon is one example.[8]

8) **Exclusivity.** Cults invariably view themselves as the *only* path to salvation. Normally the "salvation" is spiritual, though, as with the LaRouchites, it can be secular. Again, this leads to arrogance, dehumanization of nonbelievers, and an "ends justify the means" mentality. The Moonies have even adopted a "spiritual" term (for internal use only) for lying and cheating in pursuit of Church goals: Heavenly Deception.

9) **Self-Absorption.** The primary focus of a cult is the cult itself. Whatever its ostensible aims, in reality a cult is overwhelmingly self-absorbed. This is particularly noticeable in the fundraising activities of cults. They frequently raise huge sums of money which they allege will be used to alleviate social problems such as alcoholism, drug abuse, homelessness, and abandoned or abused children, when in reality they spend all, or nearly all, of the money raised to support the cult. For example, in its fundraising materials, the People's Temple routinely represented itself as a do-good organization caring for abandoned children.[9]

Secular cults are every bit as self-absorbed as religious cults. Political cults have long been notorious for infiltrating social change groups and manipulating them for the benefit of the cult, often destroying the social change groups in the process. In the 1960s, the Socialist Workers Party (itself heavily infiltrated by the FBI) and the Progressive Labor Party wreaked havoc in the anti-war movement through this tactic; in the 1970s the women's movement was the target of the International Socialists and other sects; and at present the New Alliance Party and the so-called Humanist Party are busily infiltrating environmental and other progressive groups. The political lines and the names of the cults have changed, but the virus-like infiltrate/manipulate/destroy tactic remains the same.

10) **Economic Exploitation.** Cults not only exploit their own members, but, when they can manage it, nonmembers as well.[10] While this is the usual practice, it is not invariable. The Mormons provide an interesting exception. While it's true that the Mormon church exacts tithes from its members, it also operates a fairly extensive welfare system which provides a "safety net" for down-on-their-luck church members. So, it could be argued that economic exploitation of Mormons by their church is minimal. At the same time, Mormons are often despised by non-Mormons in Mormon-dominated areas because of their "sharp" business practices. Non-Mormons often feel that Mormons, because of their "chosen people" mentality, will think nothing of cheating a non-Mormon in a business transaction.

Other cults, such as the LaRouchites, Synanon and People's Temple, have taken a more direct approach to exploiting nonmembers. They routinely represent themselves — or their front groups — as doing "good work," such as fighting drugs, when in fact virtually all of the money raised is spent on the operation of the cult. Synanon fundraisers, for example, routinely represented Synanon as a drug rehabilitation program for years after it had effectively abandoned work with drug abusers.[11] The LaRouchites have gone even further and have engaged in fraud — under the guise of fighting drugs and other "good works" — on a massive scale. As a result, many of the top members of their organization, including founder Lyndon La-Rouche, Jr., were sentenced to lengthy prison terms in the late 1980s.[12]

Direct economic exploitation of members by their cults is even less subtle. Many cults, such as the People's Temple, strip their members of assets. In the People's Temple the technique was crude — members were pressured to "donate" their possessions to the church. The Church of Scientology has taken a more sophisticated approach — members are lured by widely advertised free computer personality evaluations and pay very little to take introductory courses, but then must pay much higher fees (often in the thousands of dollars) to take "advanced" Scientology courses.[13]

Another way that cults directly exploit their members is to have them work long, exhausting hours for little or no pay. Cults which employ(ed) such tactics include Synanon, People's Temple, Unification Church, Scientology, and International Society for Krishna Consciousness (Hare Krishnas).[14]

11) **Possessiveness.** For financial and other reasons, cults will often go to great, sometimes illegal, lengths to retain members. The most extreme example of this was provided by the People's Temple · Jonestown gulag, where members were physically prevented from leaving by Jim Jones' heavily armed goon squad. A less sinister example of this tendency is provided by the Church of Jesus Christ of Latter Day Saints, the Mormons. When a Mormon leaves the fold, the LDS Church *never* gives up its attempts to recover its lost sheep. It will track the apostate for decades, and it's not unusual for LDS representatives to contact former members 30 or 40 years after they left the church in an effort to talk them into rejoining.

12) **Mind Control Techniques.** These involve such measures as keeping members malnourished and in a state of exhaustion. The classic example of this was the conduct of Jim Jones' cult in its Jonestown settlement in Guyana prior to the mass murder/suicide in 1978.[15] More sophisticated methods are also used, examples being "self-criticism" (in political cults), the use of chanting and various forms of "sensory overload" in groups like the Hare Krishnas, and the use of "therapy," as in the New Alliance Party.

Another important mind control technique is the destruction of personal privacy. The Moonies, for example, normally do not even allow potential recruits at their retreats to go to the bathroom unless accompanied by a member of the cult. This is a way of never allowing new or potential recruits to regain their mental balance.

Still another important mind control technique is the humiliation and intimidation of members. In Synanon this took the form of "the game," a type of warped encounter session in which individuals were attacked by other members of the group.[16] In the People's Temple the technique was cruder, with members being, among other things, sexually humiliated in public[17] and forced to sign false statements that they had sexually molested their children.

13) **A Closed, All-Encompassing Environment.** The classic example of this is Jonestown. Almost all cults attempt to provide such an environment for at least some of their key members, and some attempt to provide it for all of their members. The less contact that members have with external reality, the more natural the hothouse environment of the cult seems, the more natural the very peculiar beliefs of the cult seem, and the more natural it seems that everyone should follow the orders of the charismatic leader or the controlling hierarchy. A closed, all-encompassing environment also makes

members totally dependent upon the cult for social support, economic support, and a sense of identity. Thus, it tends to make leaving the cult a terrifying prospect. To put it another way, cults are like
anaerobic bacteria — they thrive in the absence of cleansing breezes.

14) **Deceptive Recruitment Techniques.** Some cults routinely de-
ceive potential members, which is understandable: Most potential
recruits would not find attractive the prospect of slavishly following
the orders of a guru-figure while working 16 to 18 hours a day for no
pay. The Unification Church in particular is notorious for deceptive
recruitment tactics.[18]

The primary recruitment targets for the Moonies are unattached
young people. They usually have a member of the opposite sex approach the target and invite her/him to dinner. According to those
who have attended such dinners, no mention of Moon or the Unification Church is made. Rather, there is general talk of a "family" and
improving the world. Next follows an invitation to spend a weekend
at a retreat. Those who accept are "love bombed" (showered with
attention) by members and are invited to a longer retreat. If they
accept, they're again "love bombed," kept constantly occupied,
accompanied by a Moonie at all times, and denied adequate sleep.
And before they know it, they're selling flowers 18 hours a day for
room and board.

Another tactic of the Unification Church is the setting up of front
groups, such as the Collegiate Association for the Research of
Principles (CARP), and having members of the front groups lie
about their association with the Unification Church if asked. In the
late 1970s CARP appeared on the campus of Boise State University
and I investigated it for the school newspaper, the *BSU Arbiter*. Even
though CARP's address was the same as that of the local Unification
Church and its literature was distributed by the members of that
Church, the Moonies staunchly maintained that there was "no
connection" between the Unification Church and CARP.

Other cults also employ front groups. The LaRouchites in
particular are notorious for this practice. This amoeba-like cult splits
so often that it's difficult to follow its permutations. Some of the
names it has operated under include the U.S. Labor Party, National
Caucus of Labor Committees, Fusion Energy Foundation, the
Schiller Institute, the National Anti-Drug Coalition, and the
National Democratic Policy Committee.

15) **Manipulation of Guilt.** Many cults expertly manipulate their members through arousal of guilt feelings. Any attempt at individual assertion or resistance to the demands of the cult's leader or hierarchy is attacked as selfishness and lack of devotion to "The Cause." This technique is especially effective when applied in public. It's a powerful goad to members to "donate" their assets to the cult and to prove their devotion through self-sacrifice.

16) **Milennarianism.** In many cults, especially those which are Christian fundamentalist, members believe that the world is coming to an end. One of the most prominent milennarian cults, the Revolutionary Communist Party (RCP), is, however, secular in nature. Rather than prophesying a biblical Armageddon, the RCP prophesies a nuclear Armageddon unless, of course, it achieves power within the next few years. If members believe this, it's a powerful incentive for them to put in long, unpaid hours working for the RCP's hierarchy and its *líder máximo*, Bob Avakian.

Milennarianism also provides a powerful insight into the hold of cults over their followers. Some cults, such as the Jehovah's Witnesses, have had the bad judgment to prophesy the date of doomsday. The Witnesses have done this repeatedly, yet when the appointed days have come and gone they have always managed to retain a majority of their blindly believing followers.

17) **Violence and Harassment.** Many cults, such as Synanon, the People's Temple, and the Church of the Blood of the Lambs of God, have employed violence and even killings to intimidate and silence critics and to keep members in line. The most famous recent incident of such violence was the rattlesnake attack upon attorney Paul Morantz by members of a Synanon goon squad in 1978.[19][20]

Other cults, such as Scientology, utilize legal harassment. The Church of Scientology is notoriously litigious and has, on one occasion, gone beyond the filing of lawsuits against its critics. In that case, Church of Scientology members, including very high-ranking members of the Church's hierarchy, attempted to frame a critic, journalist Paulette Cooper, on felony bomb charges and very nearly succeeded. A Scientology agent who "befriended" Cooper during her ordeal reported to his superiors: "She can't sleep again . . . she's talking suicide. Wouldn't this be great for Scientology!"[21] Fortunately, Cooper escaped the Scientologists' plot—after years of torment —and several of those responsible for the conspiracy against her were eventually sentenced to prison terms.

But the use of violence against nonbelievers is hardly a new phenomenon. Over 100 years ago John Doyle Lee, the Mormon elder who was scapegoated and executed in 1877 for the 1857 massacre of 120 settlers (including many women and children) at Mountain Meadows, Utah, stated:

> ". . .the people in Utah who professed the Mormon religion were at and for some time before the Mountain Meadows massacre full of wildfire and zeal, anxious to do something to build up the Kingdom of God on earth and waste the enemies of the Mormon religion. . .The killing of Gentiles [non-Mormons] was a means of grace and a virtuous deed. . .
>
> "The Mormons believe in blood atonement. It is taught by the leaders, and believed by the people, that the Priesthood are inspired and cannot give a wrong order. It is the belief of all that I ever heard talk of these things. . .that the authority that orders is the only responsible party and the Danite [member of the Mormon equivalent of the KGB, the Sons of Dan] who does the killing only an instrument, and commits no wrong. . ."[22] [23]

An even older example of the bloodthirstiness of some cults was provided by the theologian and papal agent Arnold Amalric at the Beziers massacre of Albigensian heretics in 1209: "Kill them all. God will easily recognize His own."[24]

Other students of cult behavior should certainly be capable of listing additional cult characteristics; the above-listed attributes are, however, a reasonable summary of the most important distinguishing features of destructive cults.

---

1. See the bibliography for works on these groups.
2. *Prison or Paradise: The New Religious Cults*, by James and Marcia Rudin. Philadelphia: Fortress Press, 1980, p. 20.
3. See *Crazy for God*, by Christopher Edwards. Englewood Cliffs, New Jersey: Prentice-Hall, 1979, pp. 116, 138 & 171.
4. See *Prophet of Blood*, by Dale Van Atta and Ben Bradlee, Jr.
5. See *Paradise Incorporated*, by David Gerstel. Novato, California: Presidio Press, 1982, pp. 207-224.
6. Ibid., pp. 239-252.
7. Van Atta and Bradlee, op. cit. LeBaron ordered the murder of dozens of persons, mostly members of his own polygamous sect and members of rival sects. One of those he ordered killed was his own brother.
8. See Gerstel, op. cit., for examples of cult jargon and alteration of personal appearance.

9. For a close look at a cult fundraising operation see *Six Years With God: Life Inside Jim Jones's Peoples Temple*, by Jeannie Mills. New York: A&W Publishers, Inc., 1979.

10. Ibid.

11. Gerstel, op. cit., pp. 130-133. See also *Escape From Utopia: My Ten Years in Synanon*, by William Olin (Santa Cruz, CA: Unity Press, 1980) for details on Synanon's fundraising activites.

12. See *Lyndon LaRouche and the New American Fascism*, by Dennis King. New York: Doubleday, 1989.

13. See *L. Ron Hubbard: Messiah or Madman?*, by Bent Corydon and L. Ron Hubbard, Jr. (Secaucus, New Jersey: Lyle Stuart, 1987) for instances of economic exploitation of members of the Church of Scientology. See also *Barefaced Messiah: The True Story of L. Ron Hubbard*, by Russell Miller. New York: Henry Holt and Co., 1987.

14. Rudins, op. cit., pp. 31-96.

15. Mills, op. cit.

16. Gerstel, op. cit., chapter 2.

17. Mills, op. cit., pp. 252-255.

18. See *Crazy for God*, by Christopher Edwards. New York: Prentice Hall, 1979, chapters 1 through 9.

19. Gerstel, op. cit., pp. 253-278.

20. *The Light on Synanon*, by Dave and Cathy Mitchell. New York, Seaview Books, 1980, pp. 192-195.

21. Corydon and Hubbard, op. cit., p. 170. The entire affair is described in pp. 164-170.

22. Quoted in *I Was a Mormon*, by Einar Anderson. Grand Rapids, MI: Zondervan Publishing House, 1964, pp. 57-58.

23. See also *The Mountain Meadows Massacre*, by Juanita Brooks. Palo Alto, California: Stanford University, 1950; and *Massacre at Mountain Meadows*, by William Wise. New York: Thomas Y. Crowell, 1976.

24. *The Great Quotations*, George Seldes, ed. Secaucus, New Jersey: Castle Books, 1978, p. 53.

8

Is A.A. a Cult?
(conclusions)

Is Alcoholics Anonymous a cult? That's almost as difficult to answer as the question, "What is a cult?" Rather than attempt to decide whether A.A. fits the very broad definitions offered in the previous chapter—which fit many mainstream religions and political organizations as well as groups generally conceded to be cults—it seems more appropriate to determine how many of the characteristics of the destructive cults can be found in A.A.

Considering in order the 17 criteria listed in the last chapter:

1) Is A.A. religiously oriented? Unequivocally yes.

While many A.A. members would argue that A.A. is a "spiritual" organization rather than a religious one, there is little doubt that they are quibbling over semantics. This is so obvious that even the courts have noticed it. In a 1984 Wisconsin ruling (Grandberg V. Ashland County) on judicially mandated attendance at A.A. meetings, the court stated:

> "Alcoholics Anonymous materials. . . and the testimony of the witness established beyond a doubt that religious activities, as defined in constitutional law, were a part of the treatment program. The distinction between religion and spirituality is meaningless, and serves merely to confuse the issue. . ."

As well, A.A. was founded by Bill Wilson, a member of the evangelical Christian Oxford Groups, and Dr. Bob Smith (also a member of the Oxford Groups) who insisted that new members get down on their knees and pray Christian prayers with him; and during its first years A.A. (before it adopted its name) operated as part of the Oxford Groups. In Akron, birthplace of A.A., members of what was to become A.A. identified themselves as the "alcoholic squadron of the Akron Oxford Group," during A.A.'s formative years.

A.A. literature is filled with references to "God" and a "Higher Power," and the so-called Big Book's chapter, "We Agnostics," concludes with the words, "God restored us all to our right minds... When we drew near to Him He disclosed Himself to us!" Further, fully half of the 12 Steps, the core of A.A.'s program and a codification of Oxford Group principles, mention "God," "Him," or a "Power greater than ourselves." In the early days of A.A., the religious nature of the A.A. "program" as outlined in the "Big Book" was openly acknowledged. Dr. Harry Emerson Fosdick's review of the "Big Book," which A.A. submitted unsuccessfully to the *New York Herald-Tribune* and later managed to have printed in several religious periodicals, states, "the core of their whole procedure is religious." Even today a large majority of A.A. meetings are concluded with the Lord's Prayer.

In every respect, A.A.'s orientation passes the "duck" test: If it looks like a duck, waddles like a duck, and quacks like a duck, it's probably a duck. In this case the "duck" is A.A.'s religious nature.

2) Is A.A. irrational, does it discourage skepticism and rational thinking? Again, yes.

A.A.'s emphasis is purely on emotional experience ("spiritual awakening") and "overcoming" doubts enroute to spiritual "knowledge." In the "We Agnostics" chapter of the "Big Book," Bill Wilson approvingly cites a former agnostic who "humbly offered himself to his Maker—then he knew."

A.A. folk sayings are even more revealing. Two common ones are "Your best thinking got you here" and "Utilize, don't analyze." It would be hard to think of more virulently anti-intellectual epigrams. They're all too similar to the Moonie slogan, "You Think Too Much." The distance between these slogans and their more famous counterpart, "Ignorance Is Strength," from Orwell's *1984*, is frighteningly short.

Another popular A.A. saying is "Fake it until you make it." In other words, members should sit on their doubts and mouth accepted A.A. wisdom until they feel comfortable doing it, which sounds more like a recipe for brainwashing than a recipe for "spiritual awakening."

Any doubts about this matter can be quickly resolved by a visit to almost any A.A. meeting. Newcomers who express doubts are normally assailed with bits of wisdom such as those just cited, and are almost always assured that doubting leads to drinking.

3) Does A.A. have a charismatic leader? Quite simply, no, although it does have dead saints.

To his credit, Bill Wilson never sought dictatorial control of A.A., and in fact—through devising A.A.'s anarchist form of organization—did much to ensure that no individual could ever take control of A.A. Wilson was content to be a first among equals while alive, though especially toward the end of his life he was the object of unsought veneration.

At present, Bill Wilson and, to a lesser extent, "Dr. Bob" are revered by most A.A. members, and Wilson's writings have attained the status of scripture in the minds of many. But, thanks largely to Bill Wilson, there is no charismatic leader of Alcoholics Anonymous, and it is exceedingly unlikely that there ever will be.

4) Does A.A. have a hierarchical, authoritarian structure? No, absolutely not.

Thanks largely to the 12 Traditions, Alcoholics Anonymous is a model of anarchist organization. All A.A. groups are autonomous. There is no hierarchy giving orders to the members, and it is very clear that the relatively few paid staffers are there to "serve," not to rule. Significantly, the structure of A.A. is often pictured as an inverted pyramid, with the members on top and the paid staff at the bottom.

5) Does A.A. insist on submission of the individual to the "will of God"? Yes and no.

A quick reading of the 12 Steps leaves little doubt about A.A.'s position. Step 3 states, "[We] made a decision to turn our will and our lives over to the care of God," although it does add the qualifying phrase, "as we understood Him." Another important qualification is that making this decision is officially only a "suggestion," as are the other Steps.

In practice, however, at a very large majority of A.A. meetings a great deal of pressure is placed on members to embrace this and the other "suggestions." Those who do not accept the 12 Steps are frequently made to feel unwelcome at meetings. There is even a common put-down term for such members: "one-steppers." This is a bad situation, though it would be far worse but for the official A.A. positions that the Steps are only suggestions and that the only requirement for A.A. membership is a desire to stop drinking.

Another very important limiting factor is the fact that there is no charismatic leader, authoritarian hierarchy, or priest caste in A.A. to act as interpreter(s) of "God's will." There are many members who attempt to take on the priest's role, but, fortunately, thanks to A.A.'s structure and official positions, their influence is somewhat limited.

6) Is A.A. dogmatic? Unfortunately, yes.

It's difficult to label as dogmatic an organization in which the most important guiding principles (the 12 Steps) are only "suggestions." But despite this official safeguard, a great many individual A.A. members are extremely dogmatic. They regard the 12 Steps with the reverence a fundamentalist has for the 10 Commandments, and they regard the "Big Book" as a fundamentalist would the Bible.

Anyone doubting this should attend a few A.A. meetings. At most meetings even mild criticism of the Steps or "Big Book" will be met with sarcasm, anger and put-downs. For A.A. true believers, the Steps and the "Big Book" are received wisdom; they are sacred and are to be blindly followed, not questioned.

Further confirmation of A.A.'s dogmatism is provided by its attitude toward the very many alcoholics who investigate A.A. but can't stomach its program. Rather than attempt to see *why* so many alcoholics reject A.A. (remember, these are oftentimes desperate individuals urgently seeking help), and whether anything—changes in the A.A. program, development of alternative programs—can be done to help them, A.A. blames them and maintains that the reason they can't stand A.A. is their "character defects," their lack of "honesty," or their lack of a genuine desire to stop drinking. This happens in every single case. And there have been millions. To members, the A.A. program is perfect; the problem lies solely with those who reject it.

This is the attitude of a dogmatic religious sect, not that of a rational, humanistic organization concerned with the treatment of what it insists is a deadly "illness."

7) Is A.A. separatist? Yes, but only to the extent that any special interest group is separatist.

A.A. members are self-selected "alcoholics"—as opposed to the supposedly 90 percent of the population who are non-alcoholics. The more extreme outward signs of separatism—the taking of new names and the adoption of distinctive dress or other alterations in personal appearance—are, however, absent. There is some use of jargon in

A.A., but any new member can pick up virtually all of it within a few weeks.

The functions that jargon fills in A.A. are the same as in almost any other special interest group: 1) It's a convenient form of verbal shorthand; and 2) It allows members of "the club" to recognize each other. This, of course, fosters a sense of belonging in new and long-time members alike, and reinforces the sense of separation that members feel from society at large.

But while this cannot be denied, neither can it be denied that this is a very mild form of "separatism."

8) Does A.A. see itself as the exclusive holder of the truth? Unfortunately, yes — at least in regard to the treatment of alcoholism.

This has resulted in a great deal of harm including, almost certainly, the deaths of tens if not hundreds of thousands of alco-holics. While there are a few scattered and unimportant acknowl-dgements in A.A. literature that at least the occasional drunk can sober up without A.A., at the vast majority of Alcoholics Anonymous meetings newcomers are routinely told that participation in A.A. and acceptance of the A.A. "program" (basically the 12 Steps) is the *only* way to stay sober. Compounding this, the same message is frequently delivered by alcoholism "professionals" (who very often are zealous A.A. members, some with little if any medical or psychological training) and by the mass media, which uncritically relies upon these "experts" for much of its information on alcoholism.

So, it's little wonder that many alcoholics, probably a large majority, believe A.A.'s message. And it's equally unsurprising that many who want to quit drinking but can't stomach participating in A.A. then go on to drink themselves to death. They believe that continuing to drink on the one hand, or becoming pious hypocrites on the other ("Fake it until you make it"), are the only alternatives — and that drinking is the lesser of two evils.

I myself fell into that category. In 1983 I decided to quit drinking, so I went to a few A.A. meetings believing that A.A. was the only route to sobriety. I was so horrified by what I found that I decided to give up on sobriety; and I continued a pattern of excessive, destructive drinking for another two years.

Finally, in 1985, when I became desperate enough, I quit. But it's doubtful that I would have if I had continued to believe the lie that A.A. is the only route to sobriety. Fortunately, a few months before I quit, I discovered the newsletter of a secular recovery group, (American Atheists Addiction Recovery Groups—an organization which apparently is now defunct). The newsletter directly contradicted the notion that A.A. is the only escape from abusive drinking. When I read that, I felt like a huge weight had been lifted from my shoulders.

Unfortunately, that weight continues to press down upon all too many alcoholics. They believe that A.A. is the only way to get sober—and they prefer to drink themselves to death rather than submit themselves to A.A. with its religiosity, guilt, irrationality, and endless meetings.

9) Is A.A. self-absorbed? Absolutely.

In the discussion of the failure of the Washingtonian Society (a 19th-century self-help organization similar in some ways to A.A.) in *Twelve Steps and Twelve Traditions*, Bill Wilson states, "Had they been left to themselves, and had they stuck to their one goal, they might have found the rest of the answer."[1] The implication, of course, is that A.A. has *the* answer.

Because A.A. believes it has *the* answer to alcoholism, A.A. has shown a marked disinterest in the medical or physiological aspects of alcoholism. Significantly, *none* of the dozens of books and pamphlets published by A.A. deal with this very important subject. They *all* deal with A.A. itself or, in a few cases, with day-by-day ways to remain sober.

Because of its organizational principles, A.A. has never contributed a dime toward medical research on the causes and the treatment of alcoholism. Further, because Alcoholics Anonymous has *the* answer, A.A. as a whole has shown virtually no interest in alternative programs for treating alcoholism, and many A.A. members have demonstrated marked hostility toward both professional treatment and nonreligious self-help programs such as Secular Organizations for Sobriety, Women for Sobriety, and Rational Recovery.

In San Francisco, S.O.S. members who put up flyers at A.A. hangouts told me that the flyers were ripped down very quickly. (None of the flyers attacked A.A.; they simply advertised S.O.S. meetings.) One S.O.S. member told me that before finding the group he had phoned the local A.A. office to see if they could refer him to S.O.S., and the A.A. volunteer who answered told him, "I don't know how to contact them, and I wouldn't tell you if I did." The S.O.S. newsletter is filled with reports of similar and worse incidents.

What makes this especially harmful is that (as will be shown in

Chapter 9) A.A. is an effective treatment program for only a tiny fraction of alcoholics. Through its self-absorption (and the oft-trumpeted claim that A.A. is not only effective, but the *only* effective treatment program for alcoholism), A.A. is contributing *nothing* toward the understanding of alcoholism, and is engaging in a vicious game of blame-the-victim (of what it insists is an "illness") with the approximately 95 percent of alcoholics who are not members of A.A. (According to A.A., the reason they are not members of A.A. are their "shortcomings" and lack of "honesty.")

The attitudes and behavior shown by A.A. toward medical research and alternative treatment programs are not those of a rational organization dedicated to the effective treatment of alcoholism. A.A.'s attitudes and behaviors are those of a dogmatic, self-absorbed religious cult.

Another facet of A.A.'s self-absorption is seen in members' attitudes toward the high aspirations some of their number held before they joined A.A. Within A.A., members generally view such aspirations as contributing to alcoholism because they believe that lofty goals lead to frustration and feelings of failure, which in turn lead to drinking. Because of this belief, A.A. members normally offer very little encouragement of each others' interests and pursuits outside of A.A., and sometimes actively discourage non-A.A.-related aspirations. As Dr. Margaret Bean comments, "This can set up a regressive spiral in which no one suggests that a member can or should strive for anything more challenging or interesting than sobriety."[2] And the proper way to strive for sobriety is within, and only within, A.A. itself.

10) Does Alcoholics Anonymous economically exploit its members? No, absolutely not.

All donations to A.A. are purely voluntary; there are no membership dues; and A.A. even places a cap of $1000 per year on individual donations to the organization by its members; and it will not accept *any* donations by non-members. Another example of A.A.'s economically non-exploitive practices is provided by its literature: Its books are very cheaply priced, with most selling for less than half of what comparable commercially published books would sell for, and its pamphlets are freely given away at meetings.

In comparison with televangelists and money-hungry cults such as Scientology and the People's Temple, A.A. is a model of economic unselfishness.

11) Is A.A. possessive? Does it go to lengths to retain members? No, absolutely not.

A.A. makes no organizational attempts whatsoever to retain members, and individual members normally do nothing beyond making a few friendly phone calls to other members who haven't shown up at meetings for a few days. In fact, A.A.'s tendency in this area is so contrary to that of most cults that it creates serious problems for researchers attempting to gauge the effectiveness of A.A., because of the difficulty of determining membership status. In A.A., membership is purely a matter of self-definition; those who say they're members are members. Similarly, due to the extreme and unnecessary emphasis on anonymity *within* A.A., it is next to impossible for *anyone* (including researchers and service workers within A.A.) to accurately track A.A. members.[3]

12) Does A.A. employ mind-control techniques? Quite simply, no.

While A.A. is beset by stifling dogmatism and self-absorption, and does routinely employ prayer and innocuous rituals such as the chanting of "Keep coming back, it works!" at the end of meetings, these things should not be confused with mind control techniques such as exhaustion, malnourishment, and hypnotic chanting. A.A. does nothing to alter its members' consciousness beyond the serving of a mild drug (caffeine) at meetings; and, beyond admonitions, the use of low-key rituals, sacred texts, and group pressure, it does nothing to control their thoughts.

13) Does A.A. provide a closed, all-encompassing environment for its members? Again, no.

A.A. has no live-in facilities, though it does provide a social milieu into which many members plunge when first introduced to A.A. This is entirely understandable. Many newly sober alcoholics are quite lonely (often having driven off friends, lovers, and family while on the bottle), so the friendliness of A.A. is very attractive to them; in addition, A.A. provides a "safe" environment in which they won't be tempted to drink.

A.A. recommends "90 meetings in 90 days" for new members, so newcomers who follow the recommendation spend many of their waking hours at A.A. meetings. Additionally, in the larger cities there is usually at least one A.A. hangout, and there are often several clubs and other meeting places. Finally, there is an endless amount of

A.A. volunteer work available to those who want to do it—answering the office phone, making 12th-Step calls (to "carry the message" to other alcoholics), serving as meeting officers or as group service representatives, etc. So, those who want to can easily spend their entire social lives in the world of A.A. In fact, members receive much encouragement to immerse themselves in this manner in "the A.A. way of life."

One anonymous member describes his plunge into the world of Alcoholics Anonymous:

> "After sixty days in the hospital, I was permitted to go back to my job...There I became an A.A. addict. I went to a meeting almost every night. I volunteered for the intergroup desk so my Saturdays were spent talking to drunks on the phone.
>
> "During this time, I progressed from closet atheist, to passive acceptance, to starry-eyed faith and entered that strange world where the creator of the universe was looking after minor problems like my sex life and auto battery.
>
> "It occurred to me one day with a jolt that I had begun a life of superstitious ritual. It was a sort of magic formula of prayers, meetings, and shallow talk that was 'keeping me sober.'"

But this is still a far cry from the closed environments of sinister cults such as Synanon, the Unification Church, and the People's Temple. A.A. uses none of the techniques of such cults—beatings, imprisonment, physical and sexual humiliation of members, mind control techniques—to keep its members in its orbit. Members of A.A. are free to come and to go as they please.

14) Does A.A. employ deceptive recruiting techniques? No, it doesn't.

In fact, A.A. does no recruiting whatsoever in the normal sense of the word, that of actively seeking new members. It could be argued that A.A. (or at least many of its members) does engage in deceptive recruiting by falsely representing itself as the only effective treatment for alcoholism. But it should be emphasized that probably most if not all of those who present A.A. in that light believe what they say, and are not engaging in deliberate deception as a recruiting ploy.

15) Does A.A. manipulate its members through guilt? Yes and no.

Guilt is inherent in A.A. dogma. It's enshrined in the 12 Steps with their references to "our wrongs," "our shortcomings," "defects of character" and a "moral inventory." But there is no guru-figure or authoritarian hierarchy to manipulate A.A.'s members no matter how guilty they might feel. So, the A.A. "program" fosters guilt in abundance, but there is no organizational manipulation of it. It should be added, though, that A.A.-induced (or reinforced) guilt does make members feel sinful and fearful, and thus tends to tie them to A.A., since temporary relief from the unpleasant feelings of guilt and fear is available at meetings.

16) Is A.A. milennarian? In short, no.

There is not a trace of milennarianism in A.A.

17) Does A.A. employ violence and harassment of critics and dissident members? No, absolutely not.

The use of violence by Alcoholics Anonymous is so contrary to A.A. traditions as to be unthinkable. To the best of my knowledge the relatively few incidents of harassment directed against groups such as S.O.S., which are often perceived as rivals to A.A., have been mild—verbal rudeness and the ripping down of flyers—and all of them have been committed by over-zealous individual A.A. members. As far as I know, not a single incident of harassment of "rival" groups or outside critics has been committed by a paid A.A. service worker.

The case of dissidents within A.A. is somewhat different. Within the organization, dissident members are very much second class citizens; they're often scorned and belittled; and they've found it virtually impossible to have their views presented in A.A.'s literature. But these things are as nothing compared with the vicious violence and harassment employed by many cults.

Is Alcoholics Anonymous a cult? No, though it does have dangerous, cult-like tendencies. The ideological system of A.A. is that of a cult: A.A. is religiously oriented, self-absorbed, irrational, dogmatic, insists on the submission of the individual to the will of God, and views itself as the exclusive holder of truth (at least in regard to the treatment of alcoholism).

A.A., however, has neither a charismatic leader nor an authoritarian hierarchy. It doesn't economically exploit its members. It doesn't employ mind-control techniques. It doesn't provide a closed, all-encompassing environment for members (though it does provide a social milieu within which many immerse themselves). It doesn't employ deceptive recruiting techniques. It isn't separatist in any significant sense. It doesn't manipulate its members through guilt (at least not for the purpose of exploiting them). It isn't milennarian. And it does not employ violence or harassment against critics or dissidents. To put it another way, Alcoholics Anonymous is a non-denominational religious fellowship which in all likelihood would have become a cult by now but for its anarchist organizational principles and the integrity of its co-founders.

A good indication that this is true can be found in Synanon, which started its existence as an A.A. group. Synanon broke away from A.A. in 1958 and quickly became a large and respected drug and alcohol rehabilitation organization. Two of its differences with A.A. were obvious from the start: It was a live-in organization and it had a charismatic leader, Charles Dederich, who called the shots. Predictably, within a few years of the start of its explosive growth, Synanon had developed into a cult with a closed, all-encompassing environment, and Dederich had become drunk with power. In the early 1970s Synanon declared itself a church, and about the same time the already ugly situation within the group became ever more bizarre and menacing, with mass vasectomies, head-shavings, beatings of both outsiders and would-be runaways from within the group, and, eventually, attempted murder of critics. Had Alcoholics Anonymous been founded by (or had it early—before the 12 Traditions were adopted and before the General Service Conference structure was in place—come under the control of) a sinister figure like Chuck Dederich, rather than the in many ways admirable Bill Wilson and Dr. Bob Smith, it's certainly conceivable that A.A. could have become a dangerous cult like Synanon.[4]

---

1. *Twelve Steps and Twelve Traditions*, by Bill Wilson. New York: Alcoholics Anonymous World Services, 1982, p. 178.
2. "Alcoholics Anonymous," by Dr. Margaret Bean. *Psychiatric Annals*/5:3 March 1975, p. 10/86.
3. I use the term "unnecessary" in regard to the emphasis on anonymity within A.A. because the tradition of anonymity was originally, and wisely, intended only to apply to dealings with the media.
4. The two best sources of information on Synanon are *Paradise Incorporated: Synanon*, by David Gerstel (Novato, CA: Presidio Press, 1982), and *The Light on Synanon*, by Dave Mitchell, Cathy Mitchell, and Richard Ofshe (New York: Seaview Books, 1980). In addition to being informative, both of these books—but especially *Paradise Incorporated*—are well written and "good reads."

9

How Effective is A.A.?

"Of alcoholics who came to A.A. and really tried, 50 percent got sober at once and remained that way; 25 percent sobered up after some relapses..."
— *Alcoholics Anonymous*, p. xx

"Everything you know is wrong."   — *Firesign Theater*

Is A.A. an effective treatment for alcoholism? That seemingly simple question is far more difficult to answer than one would expect. A major problem is the difficulty of defining the terms "alcoholism" and "alcoholic." Since the terms were invented over 100 years ago, a great variety of definitions have been offered, and there is still no uniformity of opinion among the "experts" about what constitutes alcoholism nor about what constitutes an alcoholic. The safest thing that can be said is that definitions are largely arbitrary and can (and do) change over time. For example, in the first edition of the "Big Book," Bill Wilson mentions "a certain type of hard drinker. He may have the habit badly enough to gradually impair him physically and mentally. It may cause him to die a few years before his time." Wilson goes on to say that this person is not a real alcoholic because he can learn to "stop or moderate."[1] Needless to say, virtually all A.A. members, as well a very large majority of alcoholism professionals, would now label such a person "alcoholic."

Another indication of the difficulties involved in defining the word "alcoholic" can be seen in the wildly varying estimates of the number of alcoholics in the United States. In the 1986 best-seller, *The Courage to Change*, Dennis Wholely estimates that there are 20 million American alcoholics. This figure is twice as high as the figure of 10 million which is found in many professional journal articles and alcoholism reference texts published in the 1970s and early 1980s, and which is still occasionally cited. A facts sheet circulated by the NCA estimates that there are 12.1 million heavy drinkers exhibiting one or more of the signs of alcoholism. And if you accept the commonly cited figure that 10 percent of American adults are alcoholics, you arrive at a figure of roughly 18 million.

The primary reason why these estimates vary so greatly is that "alcoholism" is an elusive concept with several defining factors, the limits of which are seemingly arbitrary, with the exceptions of physical dependency and tolerance (the need to drink larger amounts than the average person in order to reach a similar state of intoxication). In addition to physical dependency and tolerance, commonly cited defining factors include level of alcohol consumption, legal problems (e.g., DWIs), psychological dependency, and family, social, psychological, and economic problems. Obviously, any definition based upon such factors must be imprecise and at least somewhat arbitrary. For example, what is the precise amount of alcohol consumption which separates the alcoholic from the social drinker? And what relation does alcohol consumption have to the other defining variables? Would someone who drank 7 ounces of alcohol per day but who had relatively minor problems in other areas be defined as an alcoholic? Would someone who drank only half that amount but had severe problems in other areas be defined as an alcoholic? It's difficult to view answers to such questions as anything other than arbitrary.

One thing that is certain is that the typical A.A. member today is different than the typical A.A. member in 1940. In the early days of A.A., members were primarily "low-bottom" alcoholics who had been hospitalized for their drinking problems, and whose drinking had had devastating effects on their lives. At present, at least a large minority, perhaps a majority, of A.A. members are "high-bottom" problem drinkers who were never physically dependent upon nor tolerant of alcohol and who still functioned reasonably well socially and economically when they quit drinking. Thus, a well-designed study of the effectiveness of A.A. today would very probably yield a different result than a similar study conducted 50 years ago would have, simply because of the differences in the makeup of both A.A.'s membership and the much-expanded pool of drinkers from which it is now drawn.

With the trend toward inclusion of those with shorter and shorter and ever-less-serious drinking problems in A.A., the composition of A.A.'s membership will very likely continue to change for some time to come. (According to A.A.'s 1989 membership survey, 3 percent of A.A.'s members are *teenagers*. In the 1930s, A.A.'s early members would have considered the idea of teenage "alcoholics" ludicrous.)

One question which arises from this is what percentage of A.A.'s members are now "real alcoholics"? A complicating factor is the fact that at least some disturbed persons whose primary problems are almost certainly not alcohol related are attracted to A.A. because it's an easy way to meet their social needs.

The changing makeup of A.A.'s membership is, however, a minor problem compared with several others. The most important problem is that in attempting to gauge the effectiveness of A.A. it's very difficult to tell if you're gauging results due to the A.A. program or results due to the characteristics of A.A.'s membership. There are several factors predictive of a positive outcome to alcoholism treatment — motivation, middle class status, marital stability, employment, relatively mild and short-term problems with alcohol, and absence of serious mental illness being probably the most important — with most being found in higher-than-average percentages (for problem drinkers) in A.A.'s membership; and it should be noted that these factors are predetermining factors which were operative in a great many A.A. members before they joined A.A. An indication of the importance of these predictive factors is found in an evaluation by Frederick Baekeland of different varieties of alcoholism treatment. Baekeland compared studies of four group therapy programs serving high socioeconomic status (SES — an important prognosticator of treatment outcome) patients with studies of four group therapy programs serving skid row alcoholics and other low SES patients. The improvement rates of the programs serving the skid row alcoholics were only 18 percent, 7.9 percent, 2 percent, and 0 percent, while the improvement rates of the programs serving high SES patients were 32.4 percent, 46.4 percent, 55.8 percent, and 68 percent.[2]

As is almost universally recognized in treatment literature, the most important favorable prognosticator is "motivation." Like most cliches, the truism that "once you admit you have a problem, it's half-licked," seems to have a basis in fact. Simply showing up at an A.A. meeting implies that an individual recognizes that s/he has a problem, and in itself this self-selection seems predictive of a successful outcome. Further, certain aspects of A.A. are so unpleasant — especially the religiosity, anti-intellectuality, and the gas chamber-like, tobacco smoke-filled atmosphere at many meetings — that continued attendance in itself implies a high degree of motivation, at least for non-religious and critically minded (not to mention nonsmoking) members.

Biasing factors, such as "motivation," are a serious problem, but it does seem possible to draw at least tentative conclusions about the effectiveness of Alcoholics Anonymous. A good starting point is A.A.'s most recent triennial membership survey. At the present time A.A. claims only 900,000 members[3] in the U.S. and Canada, while there are an estimated 10 to 20 million alcoholics in the U.S. alone. The population of the U.S. is about ten times that of Canada, and for the purposes of this analysis we can assume that the ratio of A.A. members to general population is about the same in the United States and Canada. Thus, there should be approximately 820,000 A.A. members in the U.S., so in all probability only 4.1 percent to 8.2 percent of the nation's alcoholics are members of A.A. And the percentage of those who reach the A.A. goal of life-long sobriety is much lower than that.

A noticeable feature of A.A. is that a large number of its members have been in the organization for a relatively short time. Based on my attendance at A.A. meetings in San Francisco, I would estimate that over 50 percent of those attending meetings in this city have been A.A. members for less than one year and, in fact, that a majority have been members for only a few months.

This estimate is more or less in line with the figures given by Bill C. in a 1965 article in the *Quarterly Journal of Studies on Alcohol*.[4] In it, he reports that of 393 A.A. members surveyed, 31 percent had been sober for more than one year; 12 percent had been sober for more than one year but had had at least one relapse after joining A.A.; 9 percent had achieved a year's sobriety; 6 percent had died; 3 percent had gone to prison; 1 percent had gone to mental institutions; and 38 percent had stopped attending A.A. What makes these numbers even more dismal than they appear is the fact that Bill C. defined a member as someone who attended 10 or more A.A. meetings in a year's time. When you take into account the "revolving door effect," it becomes apparent that far more persons attended A.A. meetings than the 393 "members" Bill C. lists. It seems quite probable that he picked the figure of 10 meetings in a year as a membership criterion because A.A.'s success rate would have been revealed as microscopic if he had used a smaller number of attendances as his membership-defining device. (It should also be mentioned that attendance at 10 meetings in itself seems to imply a fairly high degree of motivation.)

The success rate calculated through analysis of the 1989 A.A. membership survey is hardly more impressive. The summary of the membership survey indicates that only 29 percent of members have at least five years' sobriety. Using the figure of five-years' sobriety as the criterion of success, one arrives at an A.A. success rate of approximately 1.2 percent to 2.4 percent (in comparison with the total number of alcoholics in the U.S.). If success is defined as one or more years of sobriety, A.A.'s success rate improves considerably, to 2.7 percent to 5.4 percent, as, according to A.A.'s survey, 65 percent of A.A. members have been sober at least one year.

It could be argued that this is an unfair way of evaluating the effectiveness of A.A., and that only alcoholics who have investigated sobering up via A.A. should be considered. That's a reasonable argument, but it's virtually impossible to know the exact percentage of American alcoholics who have participated in A.A. Anyone who has attended many A.A. meetings can testify that droves of new-comers show up, attend one, or a few, meeting(s), and then are never seen again—the "revolving door effect." Based on the sheer numbers of such persons, it seems probable that well over 50 percent, perhaps as many as 90 percent, of the nation's problem drinkers investigate A.A. at some time during their drinking careers. In fact, A.A.'s 1989 membership survey lends support to this estimate. According to the survey, only 5 percent of those who investigate A.A. are still attending meetings one year after they first walked through the door.[5]

If success is defined as one-year's sobriety, on the face of it this 95 percent dropout rate gives A.A. a *maximum* success rate of only 5 percent; and a great many new members do not remain continuously sober during their first year in A.A., which causes the apparent A.A. success rate to fall even lower. Of course, many of the 95 percent who drop out within the first year are probably "repeaters" who have previously investigated A.A., and this would increase the apparent A.A. success rate; but at least for the present there is no way to know what percentage of the dropouts are repeaters. Additionally, at least some of the 95 percent who drop out of A.A. during their first year do manage to sober up; but to date there's no way to know what their numbers are. As well, it seems quite probable that most of those who drop out early in the program do so because they dislike and disagree with A.A., so it could be argued that most of them who attain sobriety do so in spite of, not because of, A.A.

One thing, however, is certain: An extremely high percentage of American drinkers who have been hospitalized for alcoholism or who have participated in other institutional alcoholism programs have participated in Alcoholics Anonymous. The number of patients treated for alcoholism is now close to two million annually, which (because A.A. is a part of treatment in virtually all institutional programs) is a good indication that the proportion of alcoholics who have been exposed to A.A. is very high. It should also be kept in mind that convicted drunk drivers are routinely forced to attend A.A. as a condition of probation—which pushes the percentage of alcoholics exposed to A.A. even higher. Further, in most areas A.A. is the only widely available—and widely media-promoted—alcoholism treatment program, so A.A. has a very high volume of "walk in" traffic.

But let's give A.A. the benefit of the doubt and estimate that only 50 percent of U.S. alcoholics have tried A.A. That would double the success rate calculated earlier (based on the total number of U.S. alcoholics), and it would increase to 2.4 percent to 4.8 percent of alcoholics who have investigated A.A. if the criterion of success is defined as five-years' sobriety, and 5.4 percent to 10.8 percent if the criterion is set at one-year's sobriety. (The variation is due to the widely differing estimates of the number of American alcoholics.)

In a worst case scenario, where 90 percent of the nation's alcoholics have looked into A.A., where success is defined as five or more years of sobriety, where 29 percent of A.A. members have been sober for five or more years (as A.A. indicates), and where there are 20 million alcoholics in the country, the A.A. success rate would be about 1.3 percent (and even lower than that if the criterion of success is lifelong sobriety rather than five years' sobriety). The true success rate of A.A. is very probably somewhere between these two extremes, depending, of course, on how one defines "success"; that is, A.A.'s success rate is probably somewhere between 1.3 percent and 10.8 percent (of those who have attended A.A.).

This is far from impressive, especially when compared with the rate of "spontaneous remission." Contrary to popular belief, alcoholism is *not* a progressive and incurable "disease. Several studies have been conducted on so-called spontaneous recovery by alcoholics (that is, recovery without treatment, which can refer to achievement of either sobriety or controlled drinking), and the consensus of these studies is that "spontaneous" recovery occurs in a significant percentage of alcoholics, though the calculated rates of recovery vary considerably.[6] Other consistently supported conclusions are that the rate of alcoholism among individuals past the age of 40 declines far faster than can be explained by mortality,[7] and that "spontaneous" recovery normally occurs for identifiable reasons. In many cases remission comes suddenly after a particularly dangerous or humiliating incident shocks the drinker into realization of the seriousness of his or her drinking problem.[8] In other, probably fewer, cases, recovery occurs as the result of an "existential" decision to quit based on a gradually increasing realization of the seriousness of the problem. Whatever its causes, spontaneous recovery occurs at a significant rate. One review of available literature estimated the rate of spontaneous recovery at 3.7 percent to 7.4 percent per *year*.[9] Compared with this, the above-calculated rate of recovery via A.A. is not impressive. In fact, it appears to be no better than the rate of spontaneous recovery.

But haven't there been scientific investigations of the effectiveness of A.A.? There have been, but there haven't been many. One reason for this could well be that "A.A. does not like to have researchers around,"[10] that it is highly reluctant to "open its doors to researchers."[11] Whatever the truth of these charges, to date there have only been two well-designed studies of the effectivenss of A.A.—that is, studies which have included control groups and the random assignment of subjects. Both studies indicated that A.A. is *not* an effective across-the-board treatment for alcoholism. The subjects in both studies were, however, court-referred alcoholic offenders and hence different from the general alcoholic population in certain respects. Thus one important distinguishing feature is the fact that they did not voluntarily seek treatment; they were forced to attend A.A. and the other treatments studied.

On the surface, these factors—the employment of coercion and the special-population status of alcoholic offenders—seem to lessen the credibility of the two controlled studies of A.A.'s effectiveness. But it could be argued that one factor is irrelevant and the other actually enhances the studies' credibility. If, as is commonly asserted, A.A. is a universally applicable treatment for *all* alcoholics, the makeup of the study populations shouldn't have mattered a wit as long as assignment of subjects to A.A. and control groups was truly random. And the fact that the studies' subjects were coerced into participating could well *increase* the validity of the studies' findings because a very important biasing factor, subject motivation, was eliminated, and the remaining biasing factors were spread out fairly evenly among the groups studied because of the random assignment procedure. Further, since a large number of present-day A.A. participants are coerced into attendance either by alcoholism treatment programs or the courts, through programs for DWI offenders, the populations of these studies were perhaps not as different from the general A.A. population as one might suspect.

The first of these controlled studies of A.A.'s effectiveness was conducted in San Diego in the mid-1960s.[12] In the study 301 public drunkenness offenders were randomly divided into three groups. One group was assigned to attend A.A., another to attend an alcoholism treatment clinic, and a third group, the control, was not assigned to any treatment program. All of the study's subjects were followed for at least one full year following conviction. Results were calculated by counting the number and frequency of rearrests for drunkenness. Surprisingly, the control group was the most successful of the three, with 44 percent of its members having no rearrests; 32 percent of the subjects in the clinic group had no rearrests; and 31 percent of those assigned to A.A. had no rearrests. As well, 37 percent of the members of the no-treatment control group had two or more rearrests, while 40 percent of the alcoholism clinic attendees were rearrested at least two times, and 47 percent of the A.A. attendees were arrested at least twice. While far from a definitive debunking of A.A.'s alleged effectiveness, these results are certainly suggestive.

The other controlled study of A.A.'s effectiveness was very carefully designed and conducted and was carried out in Kentucky in the mid-1970s.[13] A large majority of its subjects were obtained via the court system, and seemed to be "representative of the 'revolving door' alcoholic court cases in our cities." The study's conductors divided 197 subjects into five randomly selected groups: a control group given no treatment; a group assigned to traditional insight therapy administered by professionals; a group assigned to nonprofessionally led Rational Behavior Therapy (lay-RBT); a group assigned to professionally led Rational Behavior Therapy; and a group assigned to A.A. Length of treatment varied from 202 to 246 days, and subjects were evaluated at the end of treatment and also at three months and 12 months following its termination.

In general, the groups given professional treatment did better than the non-professionally treated groups and the control group. A significant finding, however, was that treatment of any kind was preferable to no treatment at all.

Since professional treatment is not an option for many, perhaps most, alcoholics, it's particularly important to compare the results of the A.A., lay-RBT, and control groups. Lay-RBT was clearly superior to A.A. in terms of dropout rate. During the study 68.4 percent of those assigned to A.A. stopped attending it, while only 40 percent of those attending lay-RBT sessions stopped attending them. Further, at the termination of treatment all of the lay-RBT participants who had persisted in treatment reported that they were drinking less than they were before treatment, while only two-thirds of those who had continued to attend A.A. reported decreased drinking. As well, during the final three months of treatment, the mean number of arrests was 1.24 for the lay-RBT group, 1.67 for the A.A. group, and 1.79 for the control group. Perhaps most interestingly, the number of reported binges at three months after termination of treatment was far higher for the A.A. group than for the lay-RBT or control groups. The mean number of reported binges by the A.A. attendees was 2.37 over the previous three months, while the mean number reported by the controls was 0.56, and the mean for the lay-RBT group was only 0.26. This finding strongly suggests that the A.A. attendees had been affected by A.A.'s "one drink, one drunk" dogma, had accepted it, and had then proceeded to "prove" it. It should be pointed out, however, that at 12 months following the termination of treatment there were no significant differences between the A.A., lay-RBT and control groups.

A particularly interesting aspect of this study is that the relatively successful (compared with A.A. and the no-treatment controls) lay-RBT group utilized a treatment based on Rational Emotive Therapy (RET). The reason this is so interesting is that the program of Rational Recovery (R.R.), a new self-help secular alternative to A.A., is based entirely upon RET, and RET is utilized at least to some extent within Secular Organizations for Sobriety (S.O.S.), another of the new alternatives to A.A. To date, no scientific evaluations of the effectiveness of R.R. or S.O.S. have been published, but in light of the study just discussed it seems reasonable to suspect that both of them, though particularly R.R., might be more effective than A.A.[14]

Such speculation is, however, just that—speculation. What is certain is that certain types of alcoholism treatment work better than others, and some have shown very high success rates in controlled studies. For example, the Community Reinforcement Approach (CRA)—a treatment method utilizing behavioral family therapy, job-finding training (for unemployed clients), problem-solving training and social skills training—has shown extremely high success rates in two carefully controlled studies, with CRA-treated clients in one of the studies drinking on only 2 percent of days versus 55 percent of days for control-group clients; and the gains made by CRA-treated clients persisted throughout a 24-month follow-up period.[15]

It appears that even that bugaboo of abstinence advocates, controlled drinking, is an effective alternative to uncontrolled drinking or abstinence for many problem drinkers. A number of studies have indicated that a significant percentage of alcohol abusers *can* become moderate drinkers.[16] It's important to point out, though, that "one highly consistent finding is that individuals with less severe problems are more likely to succeed in achieving controlled drinking, whereas more severe alcoholics show better prognosis with abstinence."[17] That is, the chances of a problem drinker's achieving controlled drinking are inversely related to the seriousness and length of his or her drinking problem. Thus, it seems quite probable that abstinence is a preferable goal for those with long-term and serious drinking problems, especially if those problems involve (or involved) physical dependency and/or physical damage.

Attempts at controlled drinking by severe alcoholics are not, however, always a waste of time. There is some evidence that if severely alcoholic clients (of alcoholism treatment programs) are presented with a final opportunity to attempt controlled drinking as a treatment option, most will respond better to abstinence-oriented treatment (after their controlled drinking attempt fails) than they would have if originally presented with abstinence as the only option. This and the success of CRA and other not-widely employed treatment approaches should be seen as encouraging developments by all but those who are more committed to dogma and particular programs than they are to helping people.

It's very interesting to note that two prominent alcoholism treatment researchers, William R. Miller and Nick Heather, state that there is virtually no overlap between alcoholism treatments known to be effective and those which are widely employed. Treatments which they list as "currently supported by controlled outcome research" are aversion therapies, behavioral self-control training (controlled drinking and drink refusal), community reinforcement approach, marital and family therapy, social skills training, and stress management. The treatment methods which they list as "currently employed as standard practice in alcoholism programs," but which are not supported by controlled research, are Alcoholics Anonymous, alcoholism education, confrontation, disulfiram (antabuse), group therapy, and individual counseling.[18]

Is A.A. totally useless as a treatment for alcoholism? Perhaps not. One of the current trends in alcoholism treatment is "client matching," that is, the matching of clients to particular treatments based upon the clients' needs, personalities, and social characteristics. Since A.A. inspires fanatical loyalty in certain members, it would be surprising if A.A. wasn't an appropriate treatment method for certain alcoholics; and it seems logical that the characteristics of those for whom A.A. is appropriate would in general match the characteristics of those already succeeding in the program.

Many studies of the characteristics of A.A. members have been conducted, and based on them one researcher comments that the typical A.A. member is "likely to be a single, religiously oriented [middle class] individual...He is not highly symptomatic, and is a socially dependent guilt-prone person with obsessive-compulsive and authoritarian personality features, prone to use rationalization and reaction formation. Finally, he is a verbal person who can share his reactions with others and is not threatened by groups of people."[19]

Two other researchers list the characteristics of successful A.A. members as "male, over forty years of age, white, middle or upper class, socially stable, . . ." binge/heavy drinker, physical dependency and loss of control when drinking, "authoritarian personality, high affiliative needs, high group dependency needs, prone to guilt, external locus of control. . .cognitive simplicity, low conceptual level . . .religious orientation. . . conformity orientation, deindividuation potential."[20]

What is striking about both of these lists is that they describe the original members of A.A. almost perfectly. This, as well as A.A.'s previously discussed overall lack of efficacy, strongly suggests that A.A. would do well to stop presenting itself as a universally effective treatment program for alcoholism and instead return to its original mission of recruiting and treating "low-bottom" "up and outers"— severely dependent, middle-aged, middle- and upper-middle-class, religious, politically conservative white males. For clearly A.A. is neither a suitable nor an effective form of treatment for the vast majority of alcohol abusers.

---

1. *Alcoholics Anonymous*, by Bill Wilson. New York: Alcoholics Anonymous World Services, 1976, pp. 20-21.

2. "Evaluation of Treatment Methods in Chronic Alcoholism," by Frederick Baekeland, in *Treatment and Rehabilitation of the Chronic Alcoholic*, Benjamin Kissin and Henri Begleiter, eds. New York: Plenum Press, 1977, p. 392.

3. In a letter of June 5, 1990 to the author, the General Service Board of Alcoholics Anonymous cited the figure of 896,033 members and 43,107 groups in the U.S. These figure agree with those in the 1989 A.A. membership survey.

4. Bill C., "The growth and effectiveness of Alcoholics Anonymous in a Southwestern City," *Quarterly Journal of Studies on Alcohol*, 26:279-284, 1965.

5. "Comments on A.A.'s Triennial Surveys." New York: Alcoholics Anonymous World Services, 1990, p. 12, figure C-1.

6. See "Recovery Without Treatment," by Thomas Prugh. *Alcohol Health and Research World*, Fall 1986, pp. 24, 71 & 72.

7. "Alcoholism as a Self-Limiting Disease," by Leslie R.H. Drew. *Quarterly Journal of Studies on Alcohol*, Vol. 29, 1968, pp. 956-967.

8. "Spontaneous Remission in Alcoholics: Empirical Observations and Theoretical Implications," by Barry S. Tuchfeld. *Journal of Studies on Alcohol*, Vol. 42, No. 7, 1981, pp. 626-641.

9. "Spontaneous Recovery in Alcoholics: A review and analysis of the available research," by R.G. Smart. *Drug and Alcohol Dependence*, Vol. 1, 1975-1976, p. 284.

10. "Is Alcoholism Treatment Effective?," by Helen Annis. *Science*, Vol. 236, April 3, 1987, p. 21.

11. Baekeland, op. cit., p. 407.

12. "A Controlled Experiment on the Use of Court Probation for Drunk Arrests," by Keith S. Ditman, George G. Crawford, Edward W. Forgy, Herbert Moskowitz, and Craig MacAndrew. *American Journal of Psychiatry*, 124:2, August 1967, pp. 160-163.

13. *Outpatient Treatment of Alcoholism*, by Jeffrey Brandsma, Maxie Maultsby, and Richard J. Welsh. Baltimore: University Park Press, 1980.

14. William London of Kent State University is currently conducting a pilot study of the effectiveness of S.O.S. The Research Institute on Alcoholism, located in Buffalo, New York, will also begin a study of S.O.S.' effectiveness in the near future.

15. *Treating Addictive Behaviors: Processes of Change*, by William R. Miller and Nick Heather. New York: Plenum, 1986, pp. 152-153.

16. Ibid., pp. 145-148.

17. Ibid., p. 159.

18. Ibid., p. 162.

19. Baekeland, op. cit., p. 406.

20. "Evaluating Alcoholics Anonymous," by Alan C. Ogborne and Frederick B. Glaser, in *Alcoholism and Substance Abuse*, Thomas E. Bratter and Gary G. Forrest, eds. New York: The Free Press, 1985, p. 186. The authors do note, however, that "evidence that some of the listed attributes are associated with A.A. affiliation is weak." From personal observation and from the observations of many other ex-A.A. members, though, I believe that Ogborne's and Glaser's list of attributes are, overall, quite accurate.

10

The Future of A.A.

What is the future of Alcoholics Anonymous? The answer lies within A.A. itself. A.A. is not a cult; neither is it a cure for alcoholism. It's a nonsectarian religious organization which is the direct spiritual descendant of Frank Buchman's Oxford Group Movement. Its program of recovery, the 12 Steps, is a codification of the Oxford Group Movement's principles of individual powerlessness, divine guidance, confession, restitution, and continuance; as well, it inherited many attitudes, tendencies, and stylistic features from the Oxford Groups, including anti-intellectuality, informality, wariness of formal organization, and a fondness for slogans and aphorisms. It also inherited one other important Oxford Group Movement tendency, and that tendency is the key to A.A.'s future: *expansionism.*

Frank Buchman and the other members of the Oxford Groups were convinced that their "way of life" was the panacea for all of the world's ills. So, their overriding goal was to persuade *everyone* to adopt that "way of life." Similarly, a great many A.A. members are equally convinced that the "A.A. way of life" (that is, following the 12 Steps) is the panacea for all alcoholics. Many go further than that and, like their Oxford Group counterparts, assert that their "way of life" is a panacea which should be adopted universally—by nonalcoholics as well as by alcoholics. One enthusiastic A.A. member put it like this: "I think we're talking about a revolution—ending war, people getting rid of their anger...I honestly think that if everyone worked the 12 steps it would change the world."[1] A most interesting aspect of this statement is that its author refers to 12-Step programs as a "revolution," just as Oxford Group members referred to their reactionary religious program as a "revolution."

Additionally, A.A. members are told to "carry this message [A.A.'s program] to alcoholics" in the 12th Step, the culminating Step of A.A.'s organizational principles. It's no surprise then, that expansionism is the hallmark of A.A.; and it's virtually certain that it will continue to be so.

This expansionist tendency is obvious in the changing composition of A.A.'s membership. As mentioned in the preceding chapter, the criteria defining an "alcoholic" (thus defining who is eligible for A.A. membership) were very restrictive in A.A.'s early days. A.A. even refused to classify as alcoholic some drinkers who showed marked alcohol-related physical deterioration. At present, anyone showing *any* level of physical dependency, let alone deterioration, is automatically labelled "alcoholic" by A.A. members, and many persons who display no physical symptoms and whose drinking problems are relatively mild and of short duration are also so labelled. Thus, the pool of potential A.A. recruits has been vastly expanded.

Another sign of expansionism can be seen in the age of A.A.'s members. In A.A.'s early days there were very few members under 30 years of age; and many members were doubtful that anyone younger that 30 *could* be an alcoholic, or at least doubtful that their problems were serious enough to cause them to quit drinking. At present, 22 percent of A.A.'s members are 30 or younger, and 3 percent of A.A.'s members are teenagers.[2] Again, the pool of potential recruits for A.A. has been greatly expanded.

While the percentage of drinkers with serious drinking problems is probably no higher now than when A.A. was formed, the percentage of drinkers labelled "alcoholic," and thus eligible for A.A. membership, is far higher now than it was during A.A.'s formative years in the late 1930s. Given the current mania for labelling nearly *everyone* an addict of some sort, it seems likely that the definition of an "alcoholic" eligible for A.A. membership will continue to broaden, though it's difficult to see how it could become much broader than it is now without labelling everyone who drinks even tiny amounts of alcohol as "alcoholic."

More evidence of A.A.'s expansionism can be found in its attitude toward coercion. In its early days, A.A. was proud of being an all-volunteer organization. Today, A.A. willingly cooperates with courts which routinely coerce drunk drivers to attend A.A., and with treatment programs which routinely coerce clients to attend meetings of this once-all-volunteer organization. Again, this vastly expands the pool of potential A.A. recruits. An idea of the importance of this source of new members can be gleaned by looking at A.A.'s 1989 membership survey — 30 percent of current A.A. members were first referred to A.A. by a rehabilitation program, a percentage which has more than doubled since 1977.

As well, a huge number of the professionals employed by both inpatient and outpatient alcoholism treatment programs are zealous

A.A. members who consider A.A. the be-all and end-all of alcohol-ism treatment. In many ways, A.A. serves *their* needs very well (though not necessarily the needs of their patients). It provides them with a program with all the answers, a program which they can "utilize" and not "analyze"; and if that program doesn't work for many patients, it's the fault of the patients' "defects of character" or "lack of honesty." So, not only does A.A. supply a ready-made program, it also supplies an excuse for treatment failures. For these reasons, A.A. will probably continue to be a part of a very large majority of treatment programs, and all-too-many inpatient programs will continue to consist of little more than a 14- or 28-day drying out period punctuated by daily A.A. meetings—with a $7,000 bill falling due at the end of "treatment."

This is a comfortable arrangement for both A.A. and the for-profit inpatient treatment clinics. The clinics provide A.A. with meeting space, a huge market for its literature, and a steady stream of new members, while A.A. provides the centers with the cheapest method of "treatment" imaginable. Given these realities, it would be surprising indeed if A.A. didn't continue to cooperate with agencies which coerce drinkers to attend its meetings, and didn't continue to be an integral part of a large majority of alcoholism treatment programs in the United States, for many years to come.

In terms of sheer numbers, A.A. has been expanding in the United States and Canada, but it's been expanding much more rapidly "overseas" (which, strange as it seems, officially includes Mexico). In 1989, for the first time in its history, A.A.'s overseas members outnumbered those in the U.S. and Canada. One area of particularly rapid expansion has been Latin America.

Given the inherent anti-political activism bias in A.A.'s program, with its inward focus, its total neglect of social factors involved in the production of alcoholism, its emphasis upon individual powerlessness, and its insistence upon divine guidance as a panacea, one can only see A.A.'s Latin American expansion as, at best, a mixed blessing. Alcohol abuse is a terrible problem in many parts of Latin America, and if A.A. helps any hispanic alcoholics to overcome their drinking problems, that's all to the good; but it's difficult to see the political quietism inherent in A.A.'s ideology as being anything other than a buttress for the inequitable social systems within which alcoholism flourishes in Latin America. Given the dimensions of the alcohol abuse problem, the lack of alternative treatment programs, the presence of repressive regimes which welcome a message of political quietism, and the religion-soaked atmosphere in these countries (a not-surprising reality in lands where social misery reigns), it seems a near certainty that, for better or for worse, A.A. will continue to expand rapidly in Latin America.

A development related to the expansion of A.A. is the proliferation of non-A.A. 12-Step groups. In 1990 there were approximately 200 non-A.A. 12-Step organizations in the United States with a total membership of, probably, somewhere between 2 million and 20 million.[3] The most familiar of these groups are Gamblers Anonymous, Narcotics Anonymous, and Overeaters Anonymous. This isn't surprising. These groups all deal with widespread real and supposed addictions, just as A.A. deals with the "addiction" of alcoholism — though whether *behavior* in the absence of a physiologically addictive agent, as in Gamblers Anonymous and Sexaholics Anonymous, can be accurately labelled an "addiction" is certainly open to question.[4]

What is surprising is that groups having nothing to do with addictions have adopted the 12 Steps as their "program." Perhaps the most extreme example is Incest Survivors Anonymous. If the A.A. "program," the 12 Steps, was truly tailored to fit the needs of alcoholics (or addicts of any sort), it would seem grotesque that it be adopted as the program for *victims* of hideous and cruel crimes. (Should victims really adopt guiding principles which emphasize that *they* should make "amends" to those *they've* "harmed," take a *moral* inventory of *themselves*, and admit *their* "wrongs"?)

But the 12 Steps are *not* tailored to fit the needs of alcoholics and addicts. In fact, they're not tailored to fit the needs of *any* particular group. But for the single mention of alcohol in the first Step, they are purely a set of religious principles advocated by Oxford Group Movement/Moral Re-Armament founder Frank Buchman and crystallized by A.A. co-founder Bill Wilson.

This fact explains a great deal. From early childhood, most persons the world over are taught that God and religious faith are the very essence of goodness; so, they're favorably inclined toward anything overtly religious, such as the 12 Steps. At least in Christian countries, most are also taught, as part of their religious training, that their problems are purely their own responsibility, the results of their sins, and that only God has the power to remove those sins. So, most people are predisposed to accept 12-Step religiosity with its insistence upon individual responsibility for alcoholism (or other "addictions"), individual helplessness, and the necessity of divine guidance.

But their inherent religiosity is only a partial explanation of the popularity of 12-Step programs. There are many other reasons for their spread. One is loneliness. Loneliness is a terrible problem in American society, and people will flock to almost *anything* which relieves it—even 12-Step meetings. In the case of A.A., this factor is undoubtedly very important in the recruitment and retention of members. Alcoholics often drive off all or almost all of those close to them, and are quite socially isolated when they finally decide to quit drinking. Thus, A.A., with its innumerable meetings, social functions, and opportunities for 12th-Step work, becomes an important —sometimes the only—social outlet for many new members. While it's uncertain whether loneliness is as potent a motivating force in drawing new members to other 12-Step groups, it is undoubtedly an important factor.

Another reason for the popularity of 12-Step programs is the prevalence of rampant psychological pain in contemporary American society. The problems which 12-Step programs presume to treat are, in many cases, all too real. Because of the absence of affordable alternative treatments, and because of the massive amount of uncritical, favorable coverage such programs receive in the media, it seems only natural that a great many people turn to 12-Step programs for help. Unfortunately, it's a virtual certainty that, for the foreseeable future, the socioeconomic system will continue to act as a human meat grinder, churning out generation after generation of emotionally damaged people replete with "addictions" and other "dependencies." If the current trends toward regressive distribution of wealth and income, and sadistic, punitive "solutions" continue— jails rather than job training, savage drug laws rather than a socially tolerant legal code, etc., etc.—it seems likely that the social meat grinder will accelerate the pace of its grisly work. As well, it seems highly probable that the mass media will continue to churn out promotional puff pieces lauding A.A. and its offshoots. So, it's a virtual certainty that these factors in the growth of A.A. and other 12-Step groups will continue to operate and could well become even more potent than they are now.

A final reason for the popularity of 12-Step groups is their antiintellectualism. As Luther Burbank once remarked, "The greatest torture in the world for most people is to think." Sadly, this appears to be true, and 12-Step programs, with their "utilize, don't analyze," "your best thinking got you here" philosophy, seem ideal social vehicles for those wishing to escape the "torture" of critical thought. For many members, especially those with the "deindividuation" potential pointed out by researchers, 12-Step group-think organizations form a comfortable herd in which they can submerge themselves. (This may sound extreme, but consider the cliched remarks of many members, often consisting almost entirely of time-worn A.A. slogans and folk sayings, at almost every A.A. meeting.) Given the miserable state of the educational system and the smothering influence of fundamentalist Christianity and other anti-intellectual religions, it seems virtually certain that the anti-intellectualism of 12-Step programs will continue to be a powerful attractive force.

What is A.A.'s future? To a great degree that will be determined by A.A.'s present members, especially those members actively involved in A.A.'s administration. For the most part, these people are quite conservative — A.A.'s service structure is staffed by members deeply imbued with A.A. tradition who love the 12-Step program just the way it is, and who would fight to keep it from changing.

This is strongly related to the religious nature of A.A.'s program. For many, probably most, A.A. members, the 12 Steps and related beliefs are articles of faith; and it would be as unrealistic to expect A.A. believers to alter their central beliefs as it would be to expect Catholics to alter theirs. Additionally, as indicated in A.A.'s *Service Manual*, approval by three-quarters of *all* registered A.A. groups would be required to make any changes in the heart of A.A.'s program, the 12 Steps. Anyone familiar with A.A. will recognize that this makes changes in the Steps, A.A.'s ideological core, utterly impossible. In spite of changes in the composition of its membership, it seems certain that as long as A.A. survives it will continue to be what it has been since its articles of faith were first published in 1939: a religiously oriented ideological fossil.

Despite ideological fossilization, it seems a foregone conclusion that A.A. will continue to expand both in the United States and abroad, not because it's an effective treatment for alcoholism — it isn't — but because its criteria for membership (that is, the criteria for "alcoholism") grow ever broader; because it's developed a symbiotic relationship with the alcoholism treatment industry; because its religiosity and implied political quietism fit snugly into the existing social order; because it addresses (however inadequately) oftentimes real problems for which, all too frequently, no free or inexpensive alternative treatment is readily available; because it's widely and uncritically promoted in the media; because it provides relief from isolation and loneliness; and because it provides a quick and easy escape from the "torture" of critical thinking and individual decision-making — in other words, A.A. provides a substitute dependency, a quick and easy escape from the personal struggle necessary to achieve true independence from alcoholism.

1. "Setting Store by Personal Recovery," by Joan Smith. *San Francisco Examiner,* December 16, 1990, p. F6.
2. "Comments on A.A.'s Triennial Surveys." New York: Alcoholics Anonymous World Services, 1990, p. 2.
3. "Going to Church the 12 Step Way," by Don Lattin. *San Francisco Chronicle*, December 17, 1990, pp. A1 & A6.
4. See *Diseasing of America*, by Stanton Peele. Lexington, Massachusetts: Lexington Books, 1989.

A
Secular Alternatives to A.A.

For over 40 years after its inception in 1935, Alcoholics Anonymous was the only national self-help organization for alcoholics. That changed in 1975 when sociologist Jean Kirkpatrick founded Women for Sobriety (WFS). Kirkpatrick founded the group because she felt that the A.A. program was designed for men and did not work well for women, an opinion which certainly seems to be grounded in reality.

One reason for A.A.'s lack of effectiveness in helping women is that in mixed groups men tend to be competitive and to dominate discussions. As a result, women feel intimidated and frustrated, and often do not do well in mixed groups such as A.A.

Another reason Kirkpatrick believes that separate meetings for men and women are necessary is that self-esteen problems in male and female alcoholics are different. She believes that recovering male alcoholics need to re-build their self-esteem, while recovering female alcoholics need to build self-esteem, something which they've never had. Thus her program is geared toward fostering self-acceptance and improving women's self-concept.

Kirkpatrick discovered her principles of recovery while she was in her mid-40s and in the early stages of sobering up following a nearly 30-year-long period of alcoholism. She had tried A.A. over a decade earlier, but it hadn't worked for her; and when she tried it again at the time she finally quit, she left it quickly because it was so "male-dominated." Left to her own devices, she began to read "everything from Ralph Waldo Emerson to Norman Vincent Peale" in search of guideposts to sobriety and self-esteem. Slowly, as her readings progressed, the periods between drinking episodes gradually lengthened, until she achieved lasting sobriety.

At that point she was a 45-year-old Ph.D.-holder without a job and with no quick prospects of finding one. Rather than go through the degrading and possibly futile process of looking for work, she decided to put her expertise in sociology and recovery from alcoholism to work, and so Women for Sobriety was born.

Kirkpatrick codified her principles of recovery into the Thirteen Statements of Acceptance, which begin with the acknowledgement that "I have a drinking problem which once had me," and the central tenet of which is "I am what I think." There isn't a trace of religiosity in the Statements. (The full set of 13 Statements is reproduced in Appendix B.)

In form, WFS meetings are somewhat similar to A.A. discussion meetings, but with several differences besides the obvious one that all participants are women. An interesting contrast is that attendance at WFS meetings tends to be smaller than attendance at A.A. meetings, and that those smaller meetings are often held in members' homes. A major difference between WFS and A.A. meetings is that WFS, believing that "the past is gone forever" and that one of its prime tasks is to help women build self-esteem, discourages drunkalogues. A final significant difference is that WFS discourages substitute addictions, such as those to caffeine and sugar, so neither coffee nor sweets are served at WFS meetings, and smoking is banned as well.

Since its founding, WFS has grown slowly but steadily and now has approximately 350 chapters and 5,000 members, most in the U.S. In 1988 WFS expanded its program to cover men in a separate organization, Men for Sobriety (MFS). Its program is essentially identical to that of Women for Sobriety. The only noticeable difference is that gender-neutral or masculine terms are used in place of feminine terms in the group's literature. At this writing MFS is established in several states and has probably a few dozen members.

The address of both Women for Sobriety and Men for Sobriety is P.O. Box 618, Quakertown, PA 18951, and the phone number for both organizations is (215) 536-8026.

The largest of the non-religious alternatives to A.A. is S.O.S. — Save Our Selves/Secular Organizations for Sobriety. Its origin dates to a magazine article, "Sobriety Without Superstition," written by Jim Christopher, which appeared in the Summer 1985 issue of *Free Inquiry* magazine. It recounted Christopher's struggle to overcome his drinking problem, and the nonreligious program he had devised to achieve sobriety. The article generated an enthusiastic response, and two years later *Free Inquiry*'s publisher, the Council for Democratic and Secular Humanism (CODESH), decided to sponsor the new nonreligious recovery program S.O.S. (Secular Organizations for Sobriety, now also called Save Our Selves).

Christopher convened the first S.O.S. meeting in November 1986 in North Hollywood, California. At the time S.O.S. didn't have an office; all it had was one weekly meeting, a telephone and an answering machine. In October 1987 CODESH began its support of the new organization, and within a few months S.O.S. began to publish its quarterly newsletter. Despite having no office, an unpaid coordinator, no literature beyond the newsletter and a few amateurishly produced flyers and brochures, S.O.S. quickly expanded into a national organization. By 1988 there were over 100 S.O.S. chapters scattered across the country, with a large number of them in Northern California. In that year S.O.S. received a boost with publication of Jim Christopher's book, *How To Stay Sober: Recovery Without Religion*. The following year S.O.S. published *Unhooked: Staying Sober and Drug Free*, Christopher's second book, which recounted the evolution of S.O.S.. In that same year, S.O.S. began the process of formally incorporating as an independent organization.

S.O.S. has no structured recovery program comparable to those of A.A., Rational Recovery, or Women for Sobriety, but it does have Suggested Guidelines for Sobriety (reproduced in Appendix B). The Suggested Guidelines can be boiled down to placing great emphasis on overcoming denial and simultaneously making sobriety one's most important priority in life. S.O.S. calls this the "Sobriety Priority." This principle emphasizes sobriety as an issue separate from all others, acknowledging the priority of sobriety on a daily basis, and accepting sobriety as a necessity. S.O.S. also stresses the importance of rational thought and the scientific study of alcoholism and addiction.

In form, S.O.S. meetings resemble nothing so much as the most informal of A.A. discussion meetings, albeit without a hint of religiosity. They're generally held in schools, hospitals, library meeting rooms, and even, occasionally, in churches. The ratio of men to women is, however, considerably different in S.O.S. than in A.A.; whereas only 35 percent of A.A. members are female, in S.O.S. women comprise over 50 percent of the membership. Another major difference between A.A. and S.O.S. is that nonreligious refugees from A.A. often show up at S.O.S. meetings and, at least at first, spend quite a bit of time complaining of the condescension, hostility, and put-downs they were subjected to at A.A. meetings. S.O.S. meeting facilitators normally recognize the value of allowing new members to vent such feelings, but generally try as quickly as possible to steer discussions back to methods of staying sober.

In function, the S.O.S. service structure seems to resemble that of

A.A. — it's there to serve, not to dictate policy to groups or individual members. It provides the newsletter, brochures, and other printed materials, and functions as a means of communication and coordination for S.O.S.' widely scattered groups and members. Another resemblance to A.A. is that S.O.S. stresses group autonomy and is wary of formal organization. Still other resemblances are that S.O.S. groups are self-supporting and decline outside support; that anyone "sincerely seek[ing] sobriety" is welcome as an S.O.S. member; and that S.O.S. "has no opinion on outside matters and does not wish to become entangled in outside controversy."

In early 1990, Jim Christopher moved to Buffalo, New York, the home of *Free Inquiry* and CODESH, where he accepted a CODESH-funded position as coordinator of the S.O.S. National Clearinghouse and began to work full time to foster the development of S.O.S. This seems to have been a powerful spur to growth, as the quantity and quality of S.O.S. printed materials have improved substantially, and at the beginning of 1991 there were 325 S.O.S. groups with a total membership of approximately 6,000. (The S.O.S. newsletter is mailed to approximately 6,000 individuals.) At this writing, S.O.S. is established in all 50 states as well as England, France, Japan, Canada, and Australia.

S.O.S. can be reached at P.O. Box 5, Buffalo, NY 14215-0005. The S.O.S. telephone number is (716) 834-2921.

The third nationwide secular alternative to A.A. is Rational Recovery (R.R.). R.R. was founded in 1985 by Jack Trimpey, a licensed clinical social worker and a recovered alcoholic. The group remained quite small until 1989, when it affiliated with the American Humanist Association, published Trimpey's book, *Rational Recovery from Alcoholism: The Small Book*, and began publishing its newsletter, *The Journal of Rational Recovery*. Since that time R.R. has been growing rapidly, but it's still smaller than either Women for Sobriety or S.O.S.

One major difference between R.R. and A.A. is that R.R.'s aim is to enable alcoholics to remain sober independently of any organization. R.R. does this by teaching alcoholics the basics of Rational Emotive Therapy (RET), which is the original form of cognitive behavioral therapy and was devised by Dr. Albert Ellis. Trimpey's book is in large part an explanation of RET principles and how they can be used to overcome the desire to drink. (A brief explanation of RET principles is included in the latter part of *The Case Against*

Religiosity, by Dr. Albert Ellis, which is reproduced in this book as Appendix C.)

A major difference between R.R. and all other self-help alcoholism treatment groups is that R.R. insists upon professional involvement in its program. All R.R. groups have a professional advisor (psychiatrist, psychologist, social worker, etc.) who assists members in learning RET techniques. Advisors are not always present at R.R. meetings, but they do attend at least occasionally. The goal of R.R. meetings is to teach members enough about RET so that they will be able to leave R.R. within a year to a year and a half and remain sober. One similarity between R.R. and other recovery groups is that, despite the assistance of mental health professionals, R.R. is free.

Because its goal is to teach members to function without it, R.R. will probably never have as many members as A.A. But, paradoxically, this could well be a sign of success, not failure. R.R.'s goal is to help its members to overcome dependency, including dependency on R.R.; hence the individuals who are R.R.'s greatest successes soon leave the organization, and R.R.'s membership figure stays relatively low. Despite this self-imposed growth limitation, R.R. is expanding rapidly and is now established in 140 cities.

In early 1991 R.R. also established the nation's first nonreligious residential alcoholism treatment program. While it is an inpatient program, it is not a detoxification program; if necessary, clients must undergo detox prior to starting R.R.'s inpatient treatment. R.R.'s 30-day program provides "Rational Milieu Therapy," which features twice-a-day group therapy focusing on the use of RET to overcome the desire to drink, and also, during the later stages of the program, training in drink refusal.

Rational Recovery can be reached at P.O. Box 100, Lotus, CA 95651, and its phone number is (916) 621-4374.

B

Secular Alternatives to the 12 Steps

The 12 Steps provide something essential to self-help programs: structure. As I noted in Chapter 5, I believe that the content of the Steps is less important than their mere existence, and that any improvements in their lives believers ascribe to the Steps are actually ascribable to the placebo effect.

As well, the A.A. Steps almost certainly drive away far more alcoholics than they attract, and as noted in Chapter 5, they induce guilt, irrationality, and other-directedness. For these reasons it seems probable that a set of steps embodying rational principles of recovery would be far more useful to recovering alcoholics than the strange melange of useful concepts and irrational religiosity offered in the 12 Steps of Alcoholics Anonymous.

Several such sets of "steps" follow. It seems inappropriate to discuss their relative merits, as the primary purpose of this book is to discuss A.A. — not the alternatives to it. As well, all of the following sets of steps contain many useful principles, and readers searching for guideposts certainly won't need to be told which of the following concepts would be useful to them.

Women for Sobriety provides a set of 13 Statements of Acceptance as its "New Life Program." This program is a codification of principles discovered by WFS founder Jean Kirkpatrick during the early period of her recovery, while in search of concepts conducive to personal growth and self-control.

1. I have a drinking (life-threatening) problem that once had me.
2. Negative emotions destroy only myself.
3. Happiness is a habit I will develop.
4. Problems bother me only to the degree I permit them to.
5. I am what I think.
6. Life can be ordinary or it can be great.

7. Love can change the course of my world.

8. The fundamental object of life is emotional and spiritual growth.

9. The past is gone forever.

10. All love given returns.

11. Enthusiasm is my daily exercise.

12. I am competent and have much to give life.

13. I am responsible for myself and for my actions.

Another set of alternative steps was written by the renowned psychologist B.F. Skinner. He first sent his set of steps to A.A. with the suggestion that they offer them to nonreligious newcomers as an alternative to A.A.'s official Steps. Skinner was apparently unaware of the near impossibility of this being done (due to A.A.'s cumbersome decision-making process in regard to literature). A.A. rejected Skinner's suggestion, and he then offered his alternative steps to *The Humanist*, where they were first published in 1987:

1. We accept the fact that all our efforts to stop drinking have failed.

2. We believe that we must turn elsewhere for help.

3. We turn to our fellow men and women, particularly those who have struggled with the same problem.

4. We have made a list of the situations in which we are most likely to drink.

5. We ask our friends to help us avoid those situations.

6. We are ready to accept the help they give us.

7. We earnestly hope they will help.

8. We have made a list of the persons we have harmed and to whom we hope to make amends.

9. We shall do all we can to make amends, in any way that will not cause further harm.

10. We will continue to make such lists and revise them as needed.

11. We appreciate what our friends have done and are doing to help us.

12. We, in turn, are ready to help others who may come to us in the same way.

Rather than provide a set of "steps" to follow, Rational Recovery provides a set of irrational concepts, "Central Ideas of Alcoholism," and their rational counterparts.

1. *I am powerless over my alcoholic cravings, and therfore not responsible for what I put in my mouth,* **instead of the rational idea that** I have considerable voluntary control over my extremities and facial muscles.

2. *In order to feel like a worthwhile person, I must stop drinking,* **instead of the rational idea that** it is *because* I am worthwhile to myself that I will decide to stop drinking and build a better life.

3. *My painful emotions and alcoholic cravings are intolerable, and therefore must be controlled by drinking alcohol,* **instead of the rational idea that** some discomfort is a necessary, inevitable, and entirely harmless part of becoming sober and remaining so.

4. *I have little control over my feelings and emotions, which are somehow forced upon me by certain persons or external events,* **instead of the rational idea that** I feel the way I think, and so have enormous control over my emotions, sorrows, and disturbances.

5. *It is a dire necessity for adults to be loved, respected, or approved of,* **instead of the rational idea that** adults do not have to get what they want including love, respect, and acceptance; rejection is just another person's opinion of my worth, one with which I may gullibly agree or rationally disagree. I choose to love myself simply because it feels better than to dislike myself. In this matter, mine is the final word.

6. *Because I have committed certain acts, or behaved offensively, or harmed someone, I should therefore moralistically blame and condemn myself and feel worthless and guilty,* **instead of the rational idea that** as a human being I am uniquely fallible, and while I may feel regrets, remorse, or sadness for my alcoholic behavior, I need not conclude that I am a worthless person.

7. *Other people should not behave poorly, and when they do they should be blamed, moralistically condemned and punished for their misdeeds,* **instead of the rational idea that** everyone makes mistakes and it makes no sense to blame others for their imperfections. For me to think others are not as they should be is a failure to accept reality. If I condemn others, I will apply similar measures to my own worth and end up with personal guilt.

8. *In order to feel like a worthwhile person, I must be competent, intelligent, talented, and achieving in all possible respects, and to fail in any significant way, such as having an alcoholic relapse, is proof of what I have always suspected and feared—that I am a defective, inferior, worthless person,* **instead of the rational idea that** doing is more important than doing well, trying is the first step toward succeeding, and accepting myself now as a fallible, yet inestimably worthwhile human being is entirely possible. Succeeding does not make me into a success, and failing doesn't make me into a failure.

9. *If "things" aren't the way I want them very much to be, then it's terrible, horrible, awful, and catastrophic,* **instead of the rational idea that** "terrible" and "awful" are magical words meaning "worse than completely bad." Since nothing can be more than 100 percent bad or *completely* unfortunate, "things" don't have to be any particular way for me to remain sober and relatively calm. If I

cannot change or control conditions, I can accept any misfortune, including, when finally necessary, death.

10. *The past is an all-important cause of my present feelings and behavior,* **instead of the rational idea that** I presently feel the way I presently think, and I act largely the way I feel. I may have learned to feel badly in years past, but I may now *change my mind* about past sorrows, losses, and disappointments.

11. *Because I am sober, I absolutely must not drink, no matter what, because one drink would lead to my downfall,* **instead of the rational idea that** as time goes by drinking appears increasingly stupid because of the obvious selfish advantages of sobriety, but, if I ever stupidly relapsed by drinking, it wouldn't be awful because I would very likely recover again—selfishly, guiltlessly, and probably very quickly.

12. *Because I am an alcoholic, I need something or someone stronger or greater than myself upon which to rely,* **instead of the rational idea that** dependency is my original problem, and it is better to start now to take the risks of thinking and acting independently. I cannot really "be" an "alcoholic," but just a person who has believed some of the central ideas of alcoholism.

13. *Because alcoholism once greatly affected my life, it will continue to affect me frequently and indefinitely,* **instead of the rational idea that** because rational sobriety is self-fulfilling, and because there is so much more to life than a constant struggle to remain sober, I can gradually close the book on that sorry chapter in my life and become vitally absorbed in activities and projects outside of myself that are unrelated to my former alcoholism.

14. *Somewhere out there, there is a perfect solution for life's problems, and until I find it, I am doomed to a life of uncertainty and turmoil,* **instead of the rational idea that** uncertainty is the spice of life, and seeking a perfect solution is silly and a waste of time. I will do better to view life as an enjoyable experiment, seeking my own pleasures and cultivating my own personal growth.

Secular Organizations for Sobriety does not have a formal alternative to the 12 Steps. It does, however, have a set of Suggested Guidelines for Sobriety:

To break the cycle of denial and achieve sobriety, we first acknowledge that we are alcoholics or addicts.

We re-affirm this truth daily and accept without reservation the fact that as clean and sober individuals, we can not and do not drink or use, no matter what.

Since drinking or using is not an option for us, we take whatever steps are necessary to continue our Sobriety Priority lifelong.

A quality of life—"the good life"—can be achieved. However, life is also filled with uncertainties. Therefore, we do not drink or use regardless of feelings, circumstances, or conflicts.

We share in confidence with each other our thoughts and feelings as sober, clean individuals.

Sobriety is our Priority, and we are each responsible for our lives and our sobriety.

A great many of the principles listed above are extremely worthwhile. There are, however, certain others which I believe should be included in a truly useful set of steps to recovery. To that end, several years ago I wrote my own alternative to A.A.'s Steps. While I now believe that the first principle is overly broad — in that it treats "alcoholism" as a unitary entity, when in fact alcohol problems and the appropriate responses to them vary tremendously — I still feel that, overall, these principles are valid and quite useful.

1. Don't pick up the first drink. There is good evidence that alcoholics metabolize alcohol differently than social drinkers. Our best option is not to drink.

2. Make the effort to obtain proper nutrition, sleep, relaxation and exercise.

3. Talk about it. Nothing, especially matters related to alcohol, should be off limits. The more sensitive and painful a subject is, the greater the need to talk about it.

4. Be honest. Only by being honest with ourselves, our families, and friends, will we gain a true understanding of ourselves, why we drank, and what we need to do to stay sober.

5. But be sensible. It's necessary to be honest with one's peers, but stupid to be honest with those who hold power over us: cops, landlords, employers, and government agencies.

6. Build mutually supportive relationships with other recovering alcoholics. It's easier to open up with others who share our problems.

7. Don't get hooked on substitute addictions. Substitutes such as heroin and religion do not cause the same physical damage that alcohol does. But, like alcohol, they prevent us from controlling our own lives.

8. Use reason. Only rationality gives us the means to understand ourselves and the world we live in. Without that understanding we remain slaves to misconceptions and have no way to see through them.

9. Develop honest mental habits. Don't adopt beliefs simply because they feel comfortable. Unsupported but comforting beliefs (I'm not *really* an alcoholic. . .) contributed to our problems with alcohol, and, if we let them, will contribute to problems in the future.

10. Get involved, especially in alcohol recovery groups. By helping others, we help ourselves.

11. Find a creative outlet. Music, art, writing, and many other activities are all more enjoyable than drinking oneself into a stupor; and they help to overcome the problem of boredom, which can lead to renewed drinking.

12. Learn to value truth for its own sake. We don't need to delude ourselves. The world isn't so horrible that we need to hide from it behind irrational beliefs.

Recovering alcoholics who adopt any of the above sets of principles will have far sturdier steps to recovery to stand upon than those provided by A.A. None of these principles are written in stone, however, and many persons will undoubtedly find it useful to mix and match concepts from the various sets. Even if *none* of the above-listed principles appeal to you, you should still be able to construct your own set of steps. It shouldn't be hard for you to come up with a far better set than that provided by Alcoholics Anonymous.

C

The Case Against Religiosity

by Dr. Albert Ellis

This article will try to make a succinct and cogent case for the proposition that unbelief, skepticism, and thoroughgoing atheism not only abet but are practically synonymous with mental health; and that devout belief, dogmatism, and religiosity distinctly contribute to and in some ways are equal to mental or emotional disturbance. The case against religiosity that I am about to make is, of course, hardly unassailable and is only presented as a firm (and undevout!) hypothesis that I believe has validity but that (like all scientific hypotheses) is tentative and revisable in the light of later substantiating or nonsubstantiating evidence. I shall try to state it so that, as Karl Popper has advocated, it is falsifiable and therefore scientific.

Before I attempt to write about the advantages and disadvantages of devout religion (or religiosity), let me try to clearly define these terms. Traditionally, the term religion has meant some kind of belief in the supernatural. Thus, Webster's New World Dictionary defines religion as: (1) belief in a divine or superhuman power or powers to be obeyed and worshipped as the creator(s) and ruler(s) of the universe; (2) expression of this belief in conduct and ritual." However, in recent years religion has also come to be defined in broader terms than this; so that the same dictionary continues: "(3) Any specific system of belief, worship, conduct, etc., often involving a code of ethics and a philosophy: as, the Christian religion, the Buddhist religion, etc. Loosely, any system of beliefs, practices, ethical values, etc. resembling, suggestive of, or likened to such a system: as, humanism is his religion."

In the following article, I shall mainly discuss two particular forms of devout religion or religiosity. The first of these is a devout or orthodox belief in some kind of supernatural religion, such as Judaism, Christianity, or Mohammedism—or pious adherence to the kind of religion mentioned in Webster's first two definitions. The second form of religiosity I shall discuss is a devout or rigid belief in some kind of secular religion (such as Libertarianism, Marxism, or Freudianism)—that is, a dogmatic, absolutistic conviction that some political, economic, social, or philosophic view is sacrosanct, provides ultimate answers to virtually all important questions, and is to be piously subscribed to and followed by everyone who wishes to lead a good life.

I shall not, then, particularly discuss Webster's third definition of religion, since when the term is used to denote a mild system of beliefs, practices, or ethical values that are not connected with any assumed higher power, and that are not believed in absolutistically, devoutly, or dogmatically by secular religionists, I do not think that this kind of "religion" leads to any special individual or social harm. So a *vague*, *general*, or *moderate* set of "religious" beliefs will not be scrutinized in this article; but only a *devout* and *pious* brand of religiosity. Stated a little differently: I shall now attempt to relate absolutistic *religiosity* rather than mild *religion* to the existence of mental and emotional health.

Although no group of authorities fully agree on a definition of the term *mental health*, it seems to include several traits and behaviors that are frequently endorsed by leading theorists and therapists. I have outlined the desirability of these "healthy" traits in several of my writings on rational-emotive therapy (RET) and they have also been generally endorsed by many other therapists, including Sigmund Freud, Carl Jung, Alfred Adler, Karen Horney, Erich Fromm, Rudolf Dreikurs, Fritz Perls, Abraham Maslow, Marie Jahoda, Carl Rogers, and Rollo May. These include such traits as self-interest, self-direction, social interest, tolerance, acceptance of ambiguity, acceptance of reality, commitment, risk-taking, self-acceptance, rationality, and scientific thinking. Not all mentally healthy individuals possess the highest degree of these traits at all times. But when people seriously lack them or when they have extreme opposing behaviors, we often consider them to be at least somewhat emotionally disturbed.

Assuming that the above criteria for mental health and a few other related criteria are reasonably valid, how are they sabotaged by a system of devout religious belief or religiosity? And how are they abetted by adherence to the principles of unbelief, skepticism, and atheism? Let us now consider these questions.

1. *Self-interest.* Emotionally healthy people are primarily true to themselves and do not masochistically subjugate themselves to or unduly sacrifice themselves for others. They tend to put themselves first—realizing that if they do not primarily take care of themselves, who else will?—as well as put a few selected others a close second and the rest of the world not too far behind.

Rather than be primarily self-interested, devout deity-oriented religionists put their hypothesized god(s) first and themselves second—or last! They are so overconcerned whether their god loves them, and whether they are doing the right thing to continue in this god's good graces, that they sacrifice some of their most cherished and enjoyable interest to supposedly appease this god. If, moreover, they are a member of any orthodox church or organization, they feel forced to choose their god's precepts first, those of their church or organization second, and their own views and preferences third.

Masochistic self-sacrifice is an integral part of most major organized religions: as shown, for example, in the ritualistic self-deprivation that Jews, Christians, and Muslims must continually bear if they are to keep their faith. Orthodox religions deliberately instil guilt (self-damnation) in their adherents and then give these adherents guilt-soothing rituals to (temporarily) allay this kind of self-damning feelings.

Pious secular religionists, instead of bowing to supernatural gods, create semi-divine dictators (for example, Stalin and Hitler) and absolutistic entitities (for example, the U.S.S.R. or the Third Reich) and masochistically demean themselves before these "noble" powers—again to the detriment of their own self-interest.

2. *Self-direction.* Mentally healthy people largely assume responsibility for their own lives, enjoy the independence of mainly working out their own problems; and, while at times wanting or preferring the help of others, do not think that they absolutely *must* have such support for their effectiveness and well-being.

Devout religionists (both secular and divine) are almost necessarily dependent and other-directed rather than self-sufficient. To be true to orthodoxies, they first must immolate themselves to their god or god-like hero; second, to the religious hierarchy that runs their church or organization; and third, to all the other members of their religious sect, who are eagle-eyedly watching them to see if they defect an iota from the conduct that their god and their churchly leadership define as proper.

If devout religiosity, therefore, is often masochism it is even more often dependency. For humans to be true believers and to also be strong and independent is well nigh impossible. Religiosity and self-sufficiency are contradictory terms.

3. *Social interest.* Emotionally and mentally healthy people are normally gregarious and decide to try to live happily in a social group. Because they want to live successfully with others, and usually to relate intimately to a few of these selected others, they work at feeling and displaying a considerable degree of social interest and interpersonal competence. While they still are primarily interested in their personal survival and enjoyment, they also tend to be considerate and fair to others; to avoid needlessly harming these others; to engage in collaborative and cooperative endeavors; at times to be somewhat altruistic; and to distinctly enjoy some measure of interpersonal and group relationships.

Devout deity-inspired religionists tend to sacrifice human love for godly love (agape) and to withdraw into monastic and holy affairs at the expense of intimate interpersonal relationships. They frequently are deficient in social competence. They spend immense amounts of time, effort, and money on establishing and maintaining churchly establishments rather than on social welfare. They foment religious fights, feuds, wars, and terrorism in the course of which orthodox believers literally batter and kill rather than cooperatively help each other. They encourage charity that is highly parochial and that is linked to god's glory more than to the alleviation of human suffering. Their altruism is highly alloyed with egotistically proving to god how great and glorious they can be as human benefactors.

Devout secular religionists are often much more interested in the propagation of absolutistic creeds (e.g., Maoism) than they are in intimately relating to and in collaboratively helping humans. Like the god-inspired religionists, their charity is exceptionally parochial and is often given only to members of their own religious group while it discriminates against members of groups with opposing creedos.

4. *Tolerance.* Emotionally healthy people tend to give other humans the right to be wrong—as I and Dr. Robert A. Harper urged in the original edition of *A New Guide to Rational Living*, which we authored in 1961. While disliking or abhorring others' *behavior*, they refuse to condemn *them*, as total *persons*, for performing their poor behavior. They fully accept the fact that all humans seem to be remarkably fallible; and they refrain from unrealistically demanding and commanding that any of them be perfect; and they desist from damning people in toto when they err.

Tolerance is anathema to devout divinity-centered religionists, since they believe that their particular god (e.g., Jehovah or Allah) is absolutely right and that all opposing deities and humans are positively and utterly false and wrong. According to orthodox religious *shalts* and *shalt nots*, you become not only a *wrongdoer* but an arrant *sinner* when you commit ethical and religious misdeeds; and, as a sinner, you become worthless, undeserving of any human happiness, and deserving of being forever damned (excommunicated) on earth and perhaps roasted eternally in hell.

The pious secular religionist, without invoking god or hell, believes that the rules and regulation of his/her group or community (e.g., the orthodox religious faction in Iran) are completely right and that, at the very least, social ostracism, political banishment, and perhaps torture and death should be the lot of any strong dissenter. Religiosity, then, by setting up absolute standards of godly or proper conduct, makes you intolerant of yourself and others when you or they slightly dishonor these standards. Born of this kind of piety-inspired intolerance of self and others come some of the most serious of emotional disorders—such as extreme anxiety, depression, self-hatred, and rage.

5. *Acceptance of ambiguity and uncertainty.* Emotionally mature individuals accept the fact that, as far as has yet been discovered, we live in a world of probability and chance, where there are not, nor probably ever will be, absolute necessities or complete certainties. Living in such a world is not only tolerable but, in terms of adventure, learning, and striving, can even be very exciting and pleasureable.

If one of the requisites for emotional health is acceptance of ambiguity and uncertainty, then divinity-oriented religiosity is the unhealthiest state imaginable: since its prime reason for being is to enable the religionist to believe in god-commanded certainty. Just because life is so uncertain and ambiguous, and because millions of people think that they cannot bear its vicissitudes, they invent absolutistic gods, and thereby pretend that there is some final, invariant answer to human problems. Patently, these people are fooling themselves—and instead of healthfully admitting that they do not need certainty, but can live comfortably in this often disorderly world, they stubbornly protect their neurotic beliefs by insisting that there must be the kind of certainty that they wrongly believe they need.

This is like a young boy's believing that he must have a kindly father in order to survive; and then, when his father is unkind, or perhaps has died, the boy dreams up a father (who may be a neighbor, a movie star, or a pure figment of his imagination) and insists that this dreamfather actually exists.

Devout secular religionists invent the "certainty" of unequivocally knowing that their special political, economic, social, or other creed is indubitably true and 'cannot be falsified. Like the superhuman-oriented religionists, they also pigheadedly refuse to accept ambiguity and uncertainty—and thereby render and keep themselves neurotically defensive and immature.

6. *Flexibility.* Emotionally sound people are intellectually flexible, tend to be open to change at all times, and are prone to take an unbigoted (or, at least, less bigoted) view of the infinitely varied people, ideas, and things in the world around them. They are not namby-pamby but can be firm and passionate in their thoughts and feelings; but they comfortably look at new evidence and often revise their notions of "reality" to conform with this evidence.

The trait of flexibility, which is so essential to effective emotional functioning, is frequently blocked and sabotaged by profound religiosity. For the person who dogmatically believes in god, and who sustains this belief with a strong faith unfounded on fact—which a pious religionist of course does—clearly is not open to many aspects of change and, instead, sees things narrowly and bigotedly.

If, for example, a man's scriptures of his church tell him that he shalt not even covet his neighbor's wife—let alone having actual adulterous relations with her!—he cannot ask himself, "Why should I not lust after this woman, as long as I don't intend to do anything about my desire for her? What is really wrong about that?" For his god and his church have spoken; and there is no appeal from this arbitrary authority, once he has brought himself to unconditionally accept it.

Any time, in fact, that people unempirically establish a god or a set of religious postulates that supposedly have a super-human origin, they can thereafter use no empirical evidence to question the dictates of this god or those postulates, since they are (by definition) beyond scientific validation. Rigid secular religionists, too, cannot change the rules that their pious creeds establish. Thus, devout Nazis cannot accept any goodness of Jews or of Gypsies, even when it can be incontrovertibly shown that such individuals performed good acts.

The best that devout religionists can do, if they want to change any of the rules that stem from their doctrines, is to change their religion itself. Otherwise, they are stuck with its absolutistic axioms, as well as their logical corollaries, that the religionists themselves have initially accepted on faith. We may therefore note again that, just as devout religion is masochism, other-directedness, intolerance, and refusal to accept uncertainty, it also seems to be synonymous with mental and emotional inflexibility.

7. *Scientific thinking.* Emotionally stable people are reasonably (not totally!) objective, rational, and scientific. They not only construct reasonable and empirically substantiated theories relating to what goes on in the surrounding world (and with their fellow creatures who inhabit this world) but they also, if they follow the teachings of RET, are able to apply the rules of logic and of the scientific method to their own lives and to their interpersonal relationships.

In regard to scientific thinking, it practically goes without saying that this kind of cerebration is antithetical to religiosity. The main requisites of the scientific method—as Bertrand Russell, Ludwig Wittgenstein, Hans Reichenbach, Herbert Feigl, Karl Popper, W.W. Bartley, Michael Mahoney, and a host of other philosophers of science have pointed out—include: (1) At least in some final analysis, or in principal, all scientific theories are to be stated in such a manner that they are confirmable by some form of human experience, by some empirical referents. (2) Scientific theories are those that can in some way be falsified. But deity-oriented religionists contend that the superhuman entities that they posit cannot be seen, heard, smelled, tasted, felt, or otherwise humanly experienced and that their gods and their principles are therefore beyond the realm of science. Pious deists and theists believe that the gods or spirits they construct are transcendent: which means, in theology or religion, that they are separate or beyond experience; that they exist apart from the material universe; that, whatever science says, they are indubitably true and real.

To devoutly believe in any of the usual religions, therefore, is to be unscientific; and we could well contend that the more devout one is, the less scientific one tends to be. Although a pious religionist need not be entirely unscientific (as, for that matter, neither need be a raving maniac), it is difficult to see how such a person could be consistently scientific.

While people may be both scientific and vaguely or generally religious (as, for example, many liberal Protestants and reformed Jews tend to be), it is doubtful whether they may simultaneously be thoroughly devout and objective. Devout secular religionists (such as fanatic believers in phrenology or reincarnation) are not necessarily driven to believe in superhuman and supernatural concepts. But they almost inevitably favor absolutistic convictions about certain other issues; and absolutism and dogma are the antithesis of science. Just about all absolutists, secular and godly, tend to flout some of the basic postulates of the scientific method.

8. *Commitment.* As I have noted on several occasions in my writing on rational-emotive therapy (RET), emotionally healthy and happy people are usually absorbed in something outside of themselves, whether this be people, things, or ideas. They seem to lead better lives when they have at least one major creative interest, as well as some outstanding human involvement, which they make very important to themselves and around which they structure a good part of their lives.

In regard to the trait of commitment, devoutly religious people may—for once!—have some advantages. For if they are truly religious, and therefore seriously committed to their god, church, or creed, they to some extent acquire a major interest in life. Pious religious commitment, however, frequently has its serious disadvantages, since it tends to be obsessive-compulsive and it may well interfere with other kinds of healthy commitments—such as deep involvements in sex-love relationships, in scientific pursuits, and even in artistic endeavors (because these may interfere with or contradict the religious commitments). Moreover, religious commitment is an absorption that is often motivated by guilt or hostility and that may consequently serve as a frenzied covering-up mechanism that masks, but that does not really eliminate, these underlying disturbed feelings. Pious god-inspired commitment, moreover, is frequently the kind of commitment that is based on falsehoods and illusions and that therefore easily can be shattered, thus plunging the previously committed individual into the depths of disillusionment and despair.

Not all forms of commitment, in other words, are equally healthy or beneficial. The grand inquisitors of the medieval Catholic church were utterly dedicated to their "holy" work and Hitler and many of his associates were fanatically committed to their Nazi doctrines. But this hardly proves that they were emotionally stable humans. In fact, a good case can be made for the proposition that although involved or passionate commitment to some cause or ideal is normally healthy and happiness-producing, devout, pious, or fanatic commitment to the same kind of cause or ideal is potentially pernicious and frequently (though not always) does much more harm than good. Both deity-oriented and secular manifestations of piousness may have distinct advantages for committed individuals. But let us not forget their enormous disadvantages, too!

9. *Risk-taking.* Emotionally sound people are able to take risks, to ask themselves what they would really like to do in life, and then to try to do this, even though they have to risk defeat or failure. They are reasonably adventurous (though not foolhardy); are willing to try almost anything once, if only to see how they like it; and they look forward to some different or unusual breaks in their usual routines.

In regard to risk-taking, I think it is fairly obvious that pious theists are highly determined to avoid adventure and to refuse to take many of life's normal risks. They strongly believe in rigid and unvalidatable assumptions precisely because they are often afraid to follow their own preferences and aims. They demand a guarantee that they will be safe and secure, come what may; and since the real world does not provide them with any such guarantee, they invent some god or other higher power that will presumably give it to them. Their invention of this deity, and their piously subjugating themselves to it, thereby confirms their view that the world is too risky and gives them a further excuse for sticking to inhibiting straight and narrow (and often joyless) paths of existence.

Devout nontheistic religionists mainly substitute dogmatic belief in some philosophy or cause for a fanatical belief in god; and they use this sacredized cause to inhibit themselves against adventure and risk-taking. Thus, pious nutritionists will under no con-

ditions risk eating white bread or sugar, even when it might temporarily do them some good. And devout adherents of cognitive therapy (including devout RETers) may not tolerate the idea that *any* feeling can be free of thought and will insist that *all* dysfunctional behaviors (such as headaches and feelings of depression) *must* be of purely ideological origin.

Enormously fearing failure and rejection, and falsely defining their own worth as humans in terms of achievement and approval, devout religionists sacrifice time, energy, and material goods and pleasures to the worship of their assumed gods or godlike philosophies, so that they can at least be sure that their god loves and supports them or that an inherent Rightness is on their side. All devout religions seem to be distinctly inhibiting—which means, in effect, that piously religious individuals sell their soul, surrender their own basic urges and pleasures, in order to feel comfortable with the heavenly helper or the indubitably correct creed that they have invented or adopted. Religiosity, then, importantly consists of needless, self-defeating inhibition.

10. *Self-acceptance.* People who are emotionally healthy are usually glad to be alive and to accept themselves as "deserving" of continued life and of happiness just because they exist and because they have some present or future potential to enjoy themselves. In accordance with the principles of RET, they *fully* or *unconditionally* accept themselves (or give themselves what Carl Rogers calls unconditional positive regard). They try to perform adequately or competently in their affairs and to win the approval and love of others; but they do so for enjoyment and not for ego gratification or for self-deification. They consequently try to rate only their acts, deeds, and traits, in the light of the goals, values, and purposes they choose (such as the goals of graduating from school or of having an enjoyable sex-love relationship); and they rigorously try to avoid rating their *self*, their *being*, their *essence*, or their *totality*.

Healthy people, in other words, unconditionally accept themselves because they *choose* to do so, regardless of how well or badly they perform and regardless of how much approval they receive from others. They distinctly *prefer* to act competently and to win others' favor; and they accordingly assess and criticize their own *behaviors* when they fail in these respects. But they don't hold that they absolutley *must* do well or be loved; and they therefore don't conclude that *they*, in toto, are good *people* when they succeed and are rotten *individuals* when they fail.

In regard to self-acceptance, it seems clear that devout religionists cannot accept themselves just because they are alive and because they have some power to enjoy life. Rather, orthodox theists make their self-acceptance quite contingent on their being accepted by the god, the church, the clergy, and the other members of the religious denomination in which they believe. If all these extrinsic persons and things accept them, then and then only are they able to accept themselves. Which means that these religionists define themselves only through the reflected appraisals of god and of other humans. Fanatical religion, for such individuals, almost necessarily winds up with lack of unconditional self-acceptance and, instead, with a considerable degree of self-abasement and self-abnegation—as, of course, virtually all the saints and mystics have found.

What about theistic religions, like Christianity, that presumably give grace to all people who accept their tenets and thereby allow all humans to accept themselves unconditionally? As far as I know, there are no theistic creeds that actually do this. The best of them—like Science of Mind—state that god (or Jesus) is all-loving and that s/he therefore always gives everyone grace or unconditional acceptance. But these theistic religions still require their adherents to believe (1) that a god (or son of god) must exist; (2) that s/he personally gives you unconditional acceptance or grace; and (3) that consequently you must believe in this religion and in its god to receive this "unconditional" grace. Unless you accept these three *conditions* of grace, you will presumably never be fully self-accepting. And these *conditions*, of course, make your accepting of yourself *conditional* rather than *unconditional*. Nonreligious philosophies, such as RET, teach that you can always choose to accept yourself just *because* you decide to do so, and require no conditions or redundant beliefs in god or religion to help you do this choosing.

Ironically, in fact, when you do decide to adopt a religious view and choose to accept yourself conditionally (because you believe in a grace-giving god or son-of-god), *you* choose to believe in this religion and *you* consequently create the grace-giver who "makes" you self-acceptable. All religious-inspired forms of self-acceptance, therefore, in the final analysis depend on *your* belief system; and they are consequently actually *self*-inspired! Even when a religion supposedly

"gives" you grace, you really *choose* it yourself, and the religious trappings in which you frame your self-acceptance consist of a redundant hypothesis (that god exists and that s/he gives you grace) that is utterly unprovable and unfalsifiable and that really adds nothing to your *own* decision to be self-accepting.

Although liberal religionists (like the followers of Science of Mind) may be largely self-accepting, devout religionists have much more trouble in gaining any measure of unconditional self-acceptance. This goes for devout secular as well as pious theistic believers. For the former cannot unconditionally accept themselves because they invariably seem to make self-acceptance (or, worse yet, ego-inflation or self-esteem) depend on their adherent rigidly to the tenets of their particular creed. Thus, fanatical Nazis only see themselves (and others) as good *people* if they are good Nazis; and if they perform non-Nazi or anti-Nazi acts (e.g., espouse internationalism or help Jews or Gypsies) they damn themselves as rotten *individuals*, who presumably deserve to suffer and die. Ku Klux Klanners, along with downing Blacks, Jews, Catholics, and others, excoriate *themselves* as worthless when they fail to live up to ideal KKK standards. Pious secular religionists, like fanatical theists, seem incapable of unconditionally accepting themselves (or others), since one of the essences of devoutness or fanaticism is to thoroughly damn and to attempt to censor and punish all those who even mildly disagree with the fanatic's view.

A special way in which devout religiosity sabotages unconditional self-acceptance is its strong tendency to encourage ego-aggrandizing or grandiosity. It is clearly self-defeating to tell yourself, "I am a good person because I have good character," or "I can esteem myself because I am highly competent." For if you give yourself this kind of ego-bolstering you make yourself highly liable to self-downing as soon as it can be shown that your character is not so good or that you are beginning, in some important way, to act incompetently.

You will do even worse if you make such self-statements as, "I am a great or noble person because I do outstandingly well at work or at art," or "Because I subscribe to this particular fine philosophy or cause I am better than you are and am indeed a superior individual!" For this kind of holier-than-thou self-rating, or arrant grandiosity, assumes that you and other people can be truly superior and godlike—and that you and they are thoroughly ordinary or worthless when they are not looking down from some kind of heavenly perch.

Devout religiosity particularly foments ego-bolstering and grandiosity. Where mild religionists think of themselves as good people because they are members in good standing of their own religious group, pious ones frequently think of themselves as utterly noble and great because of their religious convictions. Thus, pious Christians, Jews, fascists, and communists tend to deify themselves for their beliefs and allegiances; and probably devout atheists also tend to feel somewhat god-like and holy! Grandiosity is one of the most common of human disturbed feelings; and it often compensates for underlying feelings of slobhood. In fact, as Camilla Anderson, a notably sane psychiatrist, has shown, few of us would ever wind up feeling like turds if we did not start off with the grandiose assumptions that we must—yes, *must*—be noble and great.

Anyway, devout religionists are frequently attracted to and bound to their piety largely because it presumably offers them holier-than-thouness and oneupsmanship over non-religionists. And by its appeal to such disturbed individuals, devout religious creeds encourage some of the craziest kinds of thoughts, emotions, and behaviors and favor severe manifestations of neurosis, borderline personality states, and sometimes even psychosis.

11. Emotionally healthy people, it almost goes without saying, accept WIGO (what is going on) in the world. This means several important things: (1) They have a reasonably good perception of reality and do not see things that do not exist and do not refuse to see things that do. (2) They find various aspects of reality, in accordance with their own goals and inclination, "good" and certain aspects "bad"—but they accept both these aspects, without exaggerating the "good" realities and without denying or whining about the "bad" ones. (3) They do their best to work at changing those aspects of reality that they view was "bad," to accept those that they cannot change, and to acknowledge the difference between the two.

Devout theistic religionists frequently refuse to accept reality in all three of the ways just listed: (1) They are frequently sure that they see things—e.g., gods, angels, devils, and absolute laws of the universe—for which there is no confirmatory empirical data and that in all probability do not actually exist. And they refuse to see some obvious things—

such as the ubiquity of human fallibility and the overwhelming unlikelihood that any humans will ever be perfect—that almost certainly do exist. (2) They often whine and scream—and even have their gods whine and scream (as Jehovah presumably did when he turned Lot's wife into a pillar of salt for looking back at Sodom and Gomorrah) when they see something "bad." They especially indulge in childish whining and in temper tantrums when other religionists or nonbelievers refuse to see the virtues of the devout theists' favored religious dogmas. (3) Instead of working hard to change grim reality, they often pray to their god(s) to bring about such changes while they impotently sit on their rumps waiting for their prayers to be answered. When certain obnoxious things are unchangeable—such as the propensity of humans to become ill and to die—they refuse to accept these realities and often invent utopian heavens where humans presumably live forever in perfect bliss, without their suffering any kinds of affliction. Obviously, therefore, devout theists often ignore, deny, and hallucinate about reality; and the more devout they are—as the long history of religion shows—the more delusionary and hallucinatory they seem to be.

Devout nontheistic religionists—such as orthodox and closed-minded capitalists, communists, and rationalists—rarely seem to deny reality as much as do devout theists. But because they dogmatically and absolutistically follow narrow creeds, they frequently look at the world and the people in it with heavily pollyannaish and/or overly pessimistic glasses and they thereby significantly distort reality by seeing it in enormously wishful-thinking ways.

If we summarize what we have been saying, the conslusion seems inescapable that religiosity is, on almost every conceivable count, opposed to the normal goals of mental health. Instead, it encourages masochism, other-directedness, social withdrawal, intolerance, refusal to accept ambiguity and uncertainty, unscientific thinking, needless inhibition, lack of self-acceptance, and reluctance to acknowledge and deal adequately with reality. In the one area where devout religion has some advantage—that of encouraging commitment to a cause or project in which people may become vitally absorbed—it even tends to sabotage this advantage in two important ways: (1) It encourages its adherents to commit themselves to its tenets for the wrong reasons—that is, to cover up instead of to face and rid themselves of their personal insecurities. (2) It encourages a fanatic, obsessive-compulsive kind of commitment that is, in its own right, a form of emotional disturbance.

This is not to deny that for some people some of the time religious notions, even when they are devoutly and rigidly held, have some benefits. Of course they do. Devout adherence to a theistic or secular form of religion can at times motivate people to help others who are needy, to give up unhealthy addictions (e.g., to cigarettes or to alcohol), to follow valuable disciplines (e.g., dieting or exercising), to go for psychotherapy, to strive for world peace, to follow longrange instead of shortrange hedonism, and to work for many other kinds of valuable goals. Historical and biographical data abound to show this good side of religiosity. But I would still contend that on the whole religious piety and dogma do much more harm than good; and the benificent behaviors that they sometimes abet would most likely be more frequent and profound without their influence.

As a good case in point, let us take the issue of interpersonal and political war and peace. Unquestionably, many devout religionists (e.g., St. Francis and St. Theresa) have led notably unangry and loving existences themselves and many others (e.g., several of the popes) have helped in the creation of world peace. So pious religion and surcease from human aggression hardly are completely incompatible. The fact remains, however, that fanaticism of any kind, especially religious fanaticism, has clearly produced and in all probability will contine to produce enormous amounts of bickering, fighting, violence, bloodshed, homicide, feuds, wars, and genocide. For all its peace-inviting potential, therefore, arrant (not to mention arrogant) religiosity has led to immense individual and social harm by fomenting an incredible amount of antihuman and antihumane aggression. It can therefore be concluded that angerattacking and peace-loving religious views that are held undevoutly and unrigidly, as well as similar views that are held by nonreligionists and antireligionists, probably serve humankind far better than religiosity-inspired peace efforts.

Religion, then, is not all bad; and even devout religiosity has some saving graces. But on the whole and in the main? The legacy and the future of dogmatic religion seem to be indicative of considerably more human harm than good.

If religiosity is so inimical to mental health and happiness, what are the chances of unbelief, skepticism, and thoroughgoing atheism helping humans in this important aspect of their lives? I would say excellent. My own view—based on more than forty years of research and clinical work in the field of psychology and psychotherapy but still admittedly prejudiced by my personal predilections and feelings—is that if people were thoroughly unbelieving of any dogmas, if they were highly skeptical of all hypotheses and theories that they formulated, if they believed in no kinds of gods, devils, or other supernatural beings, and if they subscribed to no forms of absolutistic thinking, they would be minimally emotionally disturbed and maximally healthy. Stated a little differently: if you, I, and everyone else in the world were thoroughly scientific, and if we consistently used the scientific method in our own lives and in our relationships with others, we would rarely upset ourselves about anything—and I mean *anything!*

My view of the incompatibility of skepticism and scientific thinking with what we usually call neurosis or emotional upsetness stems from my work with rational-emotive therapy (RET), a leading school of modern psychotherapy, which I founded at the beginning of 1955, after I had become disillusioned with practicing psychoanalysis and several other modes of therapy. RET is a comprehensive or multimodal system, which investigates the cognitive, emotive, and behavioral origins of human disturbance and that therefore employs a large variety of thinking, feeling, and activity-oriented methods of understanding and alleviating this disturbance. It is most famous, however, for its cognitive or philosophic theories and practices and is the father of what is now often called cognitive or cognitive behavior therapy.

One of the main postulates of RET is that neurotic disorder largely (but not completely) does not stem from the situations or events that happen to people in their past or present lives but from their own thinking *about* these events—from the explicit and implicit ideas, attitudes, philosophies, and self-statements that they believe just prior to feeling emotionally upset. Thus, when people feel anxious, depressed, inadequate, angry, or self-pitying, they feel these ways because they almost invariably tell themselves, *and devoutly believe,* one or more irrational or self-defeating ideas. I first outlined, in my original paper on RET that I presented at the American Psychological Association convention in Chicago in 1956, ten major irrational (that is, antiempirical and illogical) beliefs that people strongly hold when they upset themselves. But I later found that these can be reduced to three basic irrationalities—and that, coincidentally enough, all three of these consist of absolutistic shoulds, oughts, and musts.

I found what Karen Horney had discovered a decade before I originated RET: that human disturbance largely comes from what she called *the tyranny of the shoulds*—or from what I call *mus*turbation. Whenever people feel distinctly anxious, depressed, hostile, self-pitying, or otherwise needlessly neurotic, whenever they behave distinctly against their own wishes and interests (as when they are addicted to procrastination, smoking, or drinking even though they very much want to forego these self-defeating behaviors), they seem to devoutly believe, explicitly and/or implicitly, one or more of these *mus*turbatory creeds: (1) "I *must* perform well and *have to* win the approval of significant others by doing so, else it's *awful* and I am a *worthless person!*" (2) "Other people *must* treat me fairly and considerately; and if they don't it's *terrible* and they are *rotten individuals!*" (3) Conditions under which I live *must* be nice and comfortable and absolutely *should* easily provide me with what I want; else life is *horrible*, I *can't stand* it, and I might just as well be dead!"

If people did not consciously and unconsciously believe any of these absolutistic, unconditional musts, shoulds, and oughts, RET clearly hypothesizes, they would feel *appropriately* sad, regretful, frustrated, and annoyed when their desires and preferences are not fulfilled. But they would rarely, if ever, feel *in*appropriately panicked, despairing, self-downing, enraged, or self-pitying. Stated differently: if human's only strongly *preferred, wished,* or *desired* goals and things that they favored and only *wanted* to avoid things they disfavored, and if they never Jehovianly *demanded, commanded,* or *necessitated* that the situations they viewed as "good" exist and those they viewed as "bad" not exist, they would not seriously disturb themselves about anything—including failure, rejection, injustice, disaster, and death. Instead, they would resolutely encounter such disadvantageous conditions; feel appropriately sad (but not horrified) about them; feel strongly determined to alleviate or eliminate them; and unwhiningly accept them when they could not change these conditons.

Assuming (as RET does) that most of what we call emotional disturbance stems from absolutistic thinking—from unconditional and dogmatic shoulds, oughts, and musts

that we tell ourselves and devoutly believe—what are the main ways to change this kind of thinking and to train ourselves to live with desires and preferences instead of with godlike commands on ourselves, on others, and on the universe? RET uses many cognitive, emotive, and behavioral methods of doing this—as I have explained in several of my books, such as *Reason and Emotion in Psychotherapy, Growth Through Reason, Humanistic Psychotherapy: the Rational-Emotive Approach, Handbook of Rational-Emotive Therapy,* and *Rational-Emotive Therapy and Cognitive Behavior Therapy.* Probably the most elegant and thoroughgoing of these RET methods is that of Disputing—which has also at times been called cognitive restructuring, cognitive therapy, self-instructional training, semantic therapy, and the use of coping statements. In RET, Disputing is synonymous with skepticism, unbelief, and the scientific method. It consists of taking your basic irrational Beliefs (iBs) or your absolutistic hypotheses about yourself, others, and the world, and actively and forcefully questioning and challenging these Beliefs, until you thoroughly surrender them and replace them with rational Beliefs (rBs).

Let me briefly explain the RET Disputing process. Suppose that at point A (Activating Event) you try for a very good job that you greatly desire, mess up during the interview process, and get rejected for the job. At point C (Consequence), you feel neurotically depressed and withdraw from all further job-seeking efforts. If you know the principles of RET, you realize that although A (Activating Event consisting of failure and rejection) contributes to C (Consequence of depression and withdrawal) it does not directly "cause" it. The more important "cause" of C is B—your Beliefs about what has transpired at A. So you look, first, for your desires or rational Beliefs (rBs) and soon find them to be: "I wish I had succeeded and got accepted for this good job, and since I failed that's quite unfortunate and frustrating. But because this isn't the only good job I might get, it isn't the end of the world. Too bad! Now let me keep looking until I get another job that I really want." You see that if you rigorously and only stick to this set of rational Beliefs (rBs) you would feel appropriately sad and frustrated—but not inappropriately and neurotically depressed and withdrawn.

You therefore, still using RET, look for your irrational Beliefs (iBs)—knowing (on theoretical grounds) that they are absolutistic and unrealistic (antiempirical). Since they usually follow similar patterns, you quickly find these irrational Beliefs: (1) "I absolutely *should* not, *must* not have failed as I did in seeking this good job?" (2) "How *awful* for me to fail (as I *must* not have done) and get rejected!" (3) "I *can't stand* failing and being rejected!" (4) "Because I failed and got rejected for this job (as I *must* not have done), and because there must be something radically wrong with me for failing, I am an *inadequate person* who will doubtless fail at getting all other good jobs; who is undeserving, in fact, of getting any really good one; and who might as well quit trying to better my position in life!"

After discovering, through the use of RET, the ABCs of your feelings of depression, inadequacy, and withdrawal when you have failed to get a job that you greatly wanted, and after clearly seeing that the As (Activating Events) contribute to the Cs (disturbed emotional and behavioral Consequences) but do not directly "cause" them, and after realizing, instead, that your iBs (irrational Beliefs about the As) more directly and importantly lead to these Cs, you then proceed to D (the Disputing of your irrational Beliefs). D (Disputing) is another name for skepticism, scientific thinking, unbelief, and the logicoempirical method of extirpating antiempirical or unrealistic dogmas. Using Disputing (or the scientific method), you vigorously challenge and eliminate your irrational Beliefs (iBs) as follows:

1. You ask yourself: "Where is the evidence that I absolutely *should* not, *must* not have failed as I did in seeking this good job?" Answer: "There is no evidence for my *should* or *must*. It probably would have been highly preferable if I had succeeded in getting this job (though it is possible, also, that it would not have been preferable but turned out badly). But no matter how *preferable* it would have been, there is no *necessity* for my preferences to be fulfilled. There is no law of the universe that says that because I greatly *want* something it *must* be granted to me. If such a law existed, then I *would have* got the job; so obviously this law does not exist. Unconditional necessities—e.g., my having to have what I distinctly desire—may be *my* law, but the world clearly does not include this rule! If I *must* not have failed to get this job, then I obviously would have got it. But, clearly, I didn't! Therefore, my *must* is contradicted by reality, and I had better change it back into a strong preference."

2. You ask yourself: "In what way is it *awful* or *terrible* for me to fail and get rejected for this highly desirable job." Answer:

"In no way! Obviously, it is distinctly unpleasant and inconvenient for me to be rejected when I really want this job. But *awful* and *terrible* do not merely mean *unpleasant* or even *very unpleasant*. *Awful* means, over and above *inconvenient*, that it is *totally* bad 100% *annoying* that I failed to get this job. But that is most unlikely, since only something like being crippled for life or being dead would be close to 100% bad. And even *that* wouldn't really be 100% bad—since I can think of things worse than that, such as being crippled for life and being in continual pain. *Awful* or *terrible* means, second, *more than* bad, *more than* completely obnoxious— but, of course, nothing that ever happens to me could be more than 100% bad! *Awful* means, third, badder than it *should* or *must* be. But however bad it is for me to lose this job, it *must* be exactly that bad—for that's the way it is! So whenever I tell myself that anything is *awful*, *terrible*, or *horrible* I am really going beyond reality and contending that just because I really don't like it, and even greatly deplore it, it *must* not exist. What rot! Whatever exists exists!—no matter how bad I personally find it."

3. You ask yourself: "Is it really true that I *can't stand* losing this job and getting rejected?" Answer: " Of course I can stand it! I may never *like* it; I may, in fact, *enormously abhor* this loss and rejection. But I can always *stand* what I don't like, unless it is literally lethal and kills me. Even then, I can stand it till I die! Thus, if a steam roller rolls over me and kills me, it is silly to tell myself, while I am still alive, "I *can't stand* it, I *can't stand* it!"—for that is exactly what I am doing until I am literally dead; standing it, bearing it. The term, 'I can't stand it!' really has no sense to it, since as long as I (or anyone else) lives, we *have to* stand whatever goes on in our lives, whether it be injustice, torture, or anything else. Only when we are dead does the phrase make any sense. And when, while still alive and kicking, I whine and scream, "I *can't stand* being rejected for this job!' I am obviously out of my foolish head. For I *am* standing it. Even if I kill myself because I lost this job, I am still *deciding* to do so and the loss of the job itself does not *make me* do so. It is not because I can't stand it that I kill myself but because I idiotically *think* I can't stand it—when, of course, I really can. So I'd better almost completely eliminate the phrases, 'I *can't stand* it!' or 'I *can't bear* it' from my thinking and my vocabularly, since they are virtually never in accordance with reality."

4. You ask yourself, "Where is it written that there must be something radically wrong with me for failing to get this job? And even if it can be shown that there is something seriously wrong with me, and that I will therefore lose other good jobs as well, where is the evidence that (a) I am an *inadequate person* who will doubtless fail at getting *all* other good jobs; (b) I am therefore undeserving of ever getting any fine position; and (c) I therefore might as well quit trying to better my position in life?" Answer: "All these ideas are only written in my deluded head. First, I can easily fail to get this job or other good jobs when there is nothing radically wrong with me, but for several other reasons (such as the competition's being very heavy or my potential bosses not wanting to hire me because I am *too* intelligent or *too* competent). Second, even if it can be shown that there is something radically wrong with me, that merely means that I am a *person who has inadequacies* and not an *inadequate person.* For an inadequate person would always and only have inadequacies; and it is most unlikely that my traits are universally *that* bad. Third, even if I frequently act quite inadequately and incompetently, that never proves that I am *undeserving* of ever getting any fine position and that some universal law of *deservingness* will absolutely prevent me from getting one. It merely proves that, statistically speaking, the probability of my getting the kind of position that I want is rather low, but that if I keep trying very hard I might well get it finally get it.

If you Dispute, and keep Disputing, your irrational Beliefs (iBs) in this manner, the theory and practice of RET says that you will rarely feel emotionally disturbed and will seldom foolishly act against your own interests; and when you do, you will quickly be able to see what you are doing to needlessly upset yourself and will be able to unupset yourself again. But let me repeat, so that there will be little misunderstanding about this!—RET does not show you how to be completely calm, serene, detached, unfeeling, passive, or resigned. As its name implies, it is a rational-*emotive* type of therapy; and it assumes that you, like practically all humans, strongly desire to remain alive and to be happy. It therefore, in many ways, helps you feel *more* than you normally would—but to feel pleasure, joy, elation, and occasional ecstasy when things are going the way you want them to go and to feel, and sometimes strongly feel, sorrow, regret, frustration, and annoyance when you are not getting what you would really want to get out of life.

The Disputing that you do when you use RET is synonymous with the scientific method of challenging or disputing unrealistic or invalid hypotheses; and it is the same kind of skepticism and unbelief that you would use if you were desirous of uprooting your (or anyone else's) devout religiosity. RET, therefore, when it is employed in the manner in which I and my close associates employ it, is equivalent to the scientific method and is one of the most powerful foes of religious piety, fanaticism, and dogma.

To sum up what I have been saying in this essay: Vague, general, or mild "religion" seems to consist of people's having some serious philosophy of life, and especially an outlook about important questions like those of ethics, death, immorality, and the origin, development, and outcome of the universe. It is sometimes (and sometimes not) connected with a belief in superhuman sources and powers. This kind of religion seems a natural part of the human condition and does not seem to be intrinsically connected to mental health: since it has not been shown that vague religionists—whether they be theists, pantheists, or humanists—are emotionally healthier or unhealthier than nonreligionists. In fact, if we talk only about vague or moderate forms of "religion," it is not clear than any thoroughhoing "nonreligionists" even exist!

Devout or pious religionists, or devotees of religiosity, seem to be distinctly different from mild religionists in that they hold to their beliefs in a distinctly dogmatic, orthodox, absolutistic, rigid, closed manner. Many of them are devoutly or piously theistic—e.g., orthodox Jews, Catholics, Protestants, Muslims, or mystics—and therefore worship divine or superhuman power(s). But many of them are devout secular religionists—e.g., fanatical communists, Nazis, liberationists, or rightwing or leftwing terrorists—who are largely or completely .1on-theistic. Devout theistic and devout secular religionists differ in some important ways; but in regard to their fanaticism and absolutism they are remarkably similar.

It is my contention that both pietistic theists and secular religionists—like virtually all people imbued with intense religiosity and fanaticism—are emotionally disturbed: usually neurotic but sometimes psychotic. For they strongly and rigidly believe in the same kinds of profound irrationalities, absolutistic musts, and unconditional necessities in which seriously disturbed people powerfully believe. When, moreover, they employ the logico-empirical methods of science, and when they fully accept (while often distinctly disliking and actively trying to change) reality, they are able to surrender their devoutness and to become significantly less disturbed. Indeed, I hypothesize, the more scientific, openminded, and straight-thinking about themselves, about others, and about the world people are the less neurotically they will think, feel, and behave. This is my major hyopthesis about the relationship between absolutistic religious belief (religiosity) and mental health. The evidence that I have found, clinically and experimentally, in support of this hypothesis (as well as the evidence falsifying the hypothesis that devout religiosity is significantly correlated with and probably causative of good mental health) seems to be most impressive. But much more investigation of this issue had better be done, since it is up to me and others to empirically bolster or disconfirm these hypotheses.

For more information about RET, write to the Institute for Rational Emotive Therapy, 45 East 65th Street, New York, NY 10021.

Bibliography

This is not a comprehensive bibliography. It contains only those sources which I found useful, or consider noteworthy for other reasons.

A.A. HISTORY & İDEOLOGY

The Jack Alexander Article About A.A. New York: Alcoholics Anonymous World Services, pamphlet No. P-12. A reprint of the March 1, 1941 *Saturday Evening Post* Article, "Alcoholics Anonymous: Freed Slaves of Drink, Now They Free Others," by Jack Alexander, which gave A.A. its first big push via the national media.

"A.A. and Religion," by Margaret Bean. *Psychiatric Annals*, March 1975, pp. 36-42. A valuable and insightful discussion of A.A.'s relationship to religion.

"Alcoholics Anonymous Principles and Methods," by Margaret Bean. *Psychiatric Annals*, February 1975, pp. 7-21. Discusses the 12 Steps as part of a "conversion experience."

"A Critique of A.A.," by Margaret Bean. *Psychiatric Annals*, March 1975, pp. 7-19. A valuable discussion focusing on the psychiatric aspects of A.A. affiliation.

The Annotated Bibliography of Alcoholics Anonymous, Charles Bishop, Jr. & Bill Pittman, eds. Wheeling, WV: The Bishop of Books, 1989. A gold mine of information compiled by two A.A. enthusiasts. Not comprehensive, but a good place to start researching any aspect of A.A.

"The Ideology of a Therapeutic Social Movement: Alcoholics Anonymous," by Leonard Blumberg. *Journal of Studies on Alcohol*, Nov. 1977, pp. 2122-2143. Useful information on A.A.'s program and its intellectual precursors.

"Alcoholics Anonymous: cult or cure?," by Arthur H. Cain. *Harper's*, February 1963, pp. 48-52. An attack on A.A. because of its religiosity and dogmatism.

"Alcoholics *Can* Be Cured—Despite A.A.," *Saturday Evening Post*, September 19, 1965, pp. 6-8. Disputes the contention that alcoholics never recover and must remain dependent upon A.A., which the author terms "a dogmatic cult."

How to Stay Sober: Recovery Without Religion, by James Christopher. Buffalo, NY: Prometheus Press, 1988. The manual of Secular Organizations for Sobriety, a secular alternative to A.A. Contains a useful discussion of why alternatives to A.A. are necessary.

"Alcoholics Anonymous: Dangers of Success," by Jerome Ellison. *The Nation*, March 2, 1964, pp. 212-214. Critical article which charges that A.A.'s headquarters has been captured by an "ultraconservative clique."

The Sober Alcoholic: An Organizational Analysis of Alcoholics Anonymous, by Irving Peter Gelman. New Haven: College and University Press, 1964. A useful sociological analysis of A.A. which contains only bare-bones information on A.A.'s history.

The Varieties of Religious Experience, by William James. New York: New American Library, 1958. In the "Big Book," Bill Wilson credited *Varieties* as the source of key A.A. concepts. In reality, this book is much less important to the formation of A.A.'s ideology than is generally believed.

The Road Back: A Report on Alcoholics Anonymous, by Howard Kessel. A truly wretched book which contains virtually no useful information. Popular with A.A. enthusiasts because of its extravagant praise of A.A.

A.A.: The Story (A Revised Edition of *Not God*), by William Kurtz. San Francisco: Harper & Row, 1988. (See *Not God*)

Not God: A History of Alcoholics Anonymous, by William Kurtz. Center City, MN: Hazelden Educational Services, 1979. An extremely detailed history of Alcoholics Anonymous by one of A.A.'s friends. Probably the single best source of information on A.A., even though it reads like what it is, a Ph.D. dissertation, and the author is uncritical of both A.A. and the Oxford Groups.

"Alcoholics and God," by Morris Markey. *Liberty*, September 30, 1939, pp. 6-7. The first national article to appear on A.A.

A.A. The Way It Began, by Bill Pittman. Seattle: Glen Abbey Books, 1988. Contains much useful information on A.A.'s early days, particularly on the treatment Bill Wilson underwent at Towns Hospital before he had his "hot flash."

"The Structure of the A.A. Fellowship," by Bill Pittman. *Alcoholism & Addiction*, Nov.-Dec. 1985, pp. 53-55. A brief but clear description of A.A.'s structure.

Getting Better, by Nan Robertson. New York: William Morrow & Co., 1988. A chatty, anecdotal insider's history of A.A. Good for "color" and "feel," not so good as a detailed history.

Becoming Alcoholic, by David R. Rudy. Carbondale, IL: Southern Illinois University Press, 1986. A detailed sociological analysis of A.A.

A Sober Faith: Religion and Alcoholics Anonymous, by G. Aiken Taylor. New York: MacMillan Co., 1960. A close-to-useless discussion by a religious enthusiast.

Bill W., by Robert Thomson. New York: Harper & Row, 1975. A moderately useful biography, based largely on Wilson's recollections, which focuses on his life until 1955, the year A.A. came "of age."

Rational Recovery from Alcoholism: The Small Book, by Jack Trimpey. Lotus, CA: Lotus Press, 1989. The manual of Rational Recovery, a secular alternative to A.A. Contains a valuable discussion of the 12 Steps.

Alcoholics Anonymous, Third Edition, by Bill Wilson. New York: Alcoholics Anonymous World Services, 1985. The A.A. bible. Useful more to those studying A.A.'s program than to those studying A.A.'s history.

Alcoholics Anonymous Comes of Age, by Bill Wilson. New York: Alcoholics Anonymous World Services, 1957. Bill Wilson's rambling history and analysis of A.A. It's disorganized, but very useful.

Twelve Steps and Twelve Traditions, by Bill Wilson. New York: Alcoholics Anonymous World Services, 1953. The "12 & 12," Bill Wilson's at-length explication of the principles outlined in the Steps and Traditions.

The A.A. Service Manual combined with Twelve Concepts for World Service, (no author listed for *Service Manual*, Bill Wilson listed as author of *Twelve Concepts*). New York: Alcoholics Anonymous World Services, 1989. Absolutely essential to understanding A.A.'s service structure.

Dr. Bob and the Good Oldtimers, (no author listed). New York: Alcoholics Anonymous World Services, 1980. A.A.'s official biography of Dr. Robert Smith, A.A.'s co-founder. An indispensable source, and fairly entertaining to boot.

Pass It On: Bill Wilson and the A.A. Message, (no author listed). New York: Alcoholics Anonymous World Services, 1984. A.A.'s official biography of A.A. co-founder, Bill Wilson. Another indispensable source, and one which is quite entertaining.

"Comments on A.A.'s Triennial Surveys." New York: Alcoholics Anonymous World Services, 1990. Very useful monograph on growth of and trends in A.A.'s membership.

THE OXFORD GROUP MOVEMENT/MORAL RE-ARMAMENT

"Buchmanism: Opiate for the Classes," by Ernest Bates. *American Mercury*, June 1939, pp. 190-197. An unenlightening denunciation of the Oxford Groups.

Social Salvation, by John C. Bennett. New York: Charles Scribner's Sons, 1946, pp. 53-59. Contains a brief, but insightful, analysis of the social and political implications of Oxford Group Movement beliefs.

These Also Believe: A Study of Modern American Cults & Minority Religious Movements, by Charles Samuel Braden. New York: The MacMillan Co., 1949, pp. 403-420. Contains a not especially useful chapter on the Oxford Groups.

The Oxford Group: Its History and Significance, by Walter Houston Clark. New York: Bookman Associates, 1951. A very sympathetic, very uncritical history and analysis of the Oxford Group Movement.

"Salvation for the Select," by Frank Devine. *American Mercury*, March 1933, pp. 313-319. Description of Oxford Group activities focusing on the economically privileged status of participants.

The Mystery of Moral Re-Armament, by Tom Driberg. New York: Alfred A. Knopf, 1965. By far the best single source of information on the Oxford Groups. Well written, well documented, and a good read.

Drawing-Room Conversion: A Sociological Account of the Oxford Group Movement, by Allan W. Eister. Durham, NC: Duke University Press, 1950. Valuable for its description and analysis of the inner workings of the Oxford Groups. One of the better works on the subject.

The Confusion of Tongues: A Review of Modern Isms, by Charles W. Ferguson. Grand Rapids, MI: Zondervan Publishing House, 1940, pp. 89-109. Contains a very entertaining account of the incidents which led to Frank Buchman's being banned by Princeton University.

The Oxford Group Movement, by Herbert Hensley Henson, D.D. (Bishop of Durham). New York: Oxford University Press, 1933. A leading clergyman's attack on the Oxford Groups for their arrogance, intolerance, and lack of social concern.

Saints Run Mad, by Marjorie Harrison. London: John Lane, The Bodley Head, 1934. A trenchant attack on Buchman's "well-fed" movement by a liberal Christian critic.

Britain and the Beast, by Peter Howard. London: Heinemann, 1963. An absolute howler written by the then-head of MRA. A piece of hysterical puritanism with chapters bearing titles such as "Guts and Grandeur," "Queens and Queers," and "Beasts and Bishops."

Not God: A History of Alcoholics Anonymous, by William Kurtz. Center City, MN: Hazelden Educational Services, 1979. Contains plentiful, if dry and apologetic, material on the Oxford Group Movement and its founder, Frank Buchman.

Personal Religion, by Douglas Clyde MacIntosh. New York: Charles Scribner's Sons, 1942, pp. 372-395. Contains an informative analysis of Oxford Group Movement ideology.

"Hitler and Buchman," by Reinhold Niebuhr. *The Christian Century*, October 7, 1936, pp. 1315 & 1316. Niebuhr's denunciation of Buchman and the Oxford Group Movement spurred by Buchman's "Thank heaven for a man like Adolf Hitler" remarks published in an interview in the *New York World Telegram*.

A.A. The Way It Began, by Bill Pittman. Seattle: Glen Abbey Books, 1988. Contains a chapter on the Oxford Groups which carefully avoids mention of anything reflecting negatively on them.

The Groups Movement, by Rev. John A. Richardson. Milwaukee: Morehouse Publishing Co., 1935. A critical analysis of the Oxford Groups focusing, among other things, on their false claims and the negative consequences of some of their practices.

"U.S. Letter: Chicago," by Calvin Trillin. *The New Yorker*, December 16, 1967, pp. 128-136. A sarcastic, very entertaining description of Up with People!, the MRA kiddie vocal group spinoff.

"Apostle to the Twentieth Century," by Henry P. Van Dusen. *Atlantic Monthly*, July 1934, pp. 1-16. A biography and analysis of Oxford Group Movement founder Frank Buchman.

"The Oxford Group Movement," by Henry P. Van Dusen. *Atlantic Monthly*, August 1934, pp. 240-252. A critical, but overall friendly, analysis of the Groups.

"Buchman's Kampf" (no author listed). *Time*, January 18, 1943, pp. 65-66. A brief account of the attempts at draft evasion by some of Buchman's followers during World War II.

"A God Guided Dictator" (no author listed). *The Christian Century*, September 9, 1936, pp. 1182-1183. An incisive, biting commentary on the political implications of Oxford Group Movement beliefs.

Ideology and Co-Existence (no author listed). Moral Re-Armament, 1959. A prime example of MRA megalomania and Cold War hysteria.

"Less Buchmanism" (no author listed). *Time*, November 24, 1941. A brief piece on the declining fortunes of the Oxford Groups during the opening days of World War II.

"New Man at M.R.A." (no author listed). *Time*, October 30, 1964, p. 74. A brief biography of Frank Buchman's successor as the head of Moral Re-Armament, Peter Howard.

"Moral Re-Armament RIP" (no author listed). *National Review*, October 20, 1970, p. 1099. A very brief description of the disintegration of MRA in the U.S.

"The Moral Re-Armer" (no author listed). *Time*, August 18, 1961, p. 59. A brief obituary of Frank Buchman.

"Oxford Group: God-Guidance and Four 'Absolute' Principles" (no author listed). *Newsweek*, June 6, 1936, pp. 26-27. A very useful account of a large houseparty and the state of Buchman's movement at the height of its popularity.

"The Oxford Group—Genuine or a Mockery?" (no author listed). *Literary Digest*, January 28, 1933, pp. 18-19. A brief description which is fairly critical.

"Report on Buchmanism" (no author listed). *Time*, January 4, 1943, p. 68. A brief report on the decline of the Oxford Group Movement during World War II.

"When the White Begins to Fade" (no author listed). *The Christian Century*, June 28, 1972, pp. 704-705. A brief piece on the declining fortunes of Moral Re-Armament in Britain.

EFFECTIVENESS OF A.A.

"Is Alcoholism Treatment Effective?," by Helen Annis. *Science*, April 3, 1987, pp. 20-22. Not as useful as the title would suggest, but not bad for a short overview.

Alcoholism and Treatment, by David J. Armor, J. Michael Polich, & Harriet B. Stambul. New York: John Wiley & Sons, 1978. Contains a brief section on A.A. as an adjunct to clinic treatment.

"Evaluation of Treatment Methods in Chronic Alcoholism," by Frederick Baekeland. Chapter 10, pp. 385-440 in *Treatment and Rehabilitation of the Chronic Alcoholic*, Benjamin Kissin and Henri Begleiter, eds. New York: Plenum Press, 1977. A comprehensive comparison of all commonly employed treatment methods. Now slightly dated, but still extremely useful. Also published as Chapter 7, "Methods for the Treatment of Chronic Alcoholism: A Critical Appraisal," of *Research Advances in Alcohol and Drug Problems, Vol. 2*, Robert Gibbins et al, eds. New York: John Wiley & Sons, 1975, pp. 247-327.

"The Efficacy of Alcoholics Anonymous: The Elusiveness of Hard Data," by Paul E. Bebbington. *British Journal of Psychiatry*, Vol. 128 (1976), pp. 572-580. Very thorough discussion of the defects of research conducted on A.A.'s effectiveness as a treatment method.

The Annotated Bibliography of Alcoholics Anonymous, Charles Bishop, Jr. & Bill Pittman, eds. Wheeling, WV: The Bishop of Books, 1989. A gold mine of information compiled by two A.A. enthusiasts. Not comprehensive, but a good place to start researching any aspect of A.A.

Outpatient Treatment of Alcoholism, by Jeffrey M. Brandsma, Maxie C. Maultsby, Jr., & Richard J. Welsh. Baltimore: University Park Press, 1980. A very detailed and technical book-length report on the best controlled study of A.A.'s effectiveness conducted to date. Indispensable.

"The Growth and Effectiveness of Alcoholics Anonymous in a Southwestern City, 1945-1962," by Bill C. *Quarterly Journal of Studies on Alcohol*, 26:279-284, 1965. The first longitudinal study of A.A. membership, and one conducted by an A.A. member. Unfortunately, due to severe design flaws, the data provided by this study is of very limited use.

Understanding America's Drinking Problem, by Dennis Cahalan. San Francisco: Jossey-Bass, 1987. A general overview more useful to the uninformed than to the serious researcher.

"Relapse Prevention with Substance Abusers: Clinical Issues and Myths," by Dennis C. Daley. *Social Work*, March-April 1987, pp. 138-142. Discusses reasons for relapse, including A.A.'s self-fulfilling prophecy, "One drink, one drunk."

"A Controlled Experiment on the Use of Court Probation for Drunk Arrests," by Keith Ditman, George Crawford, Edward Forby, Herbert Moskowitz & Craig MacAndrew. *American Journal of Psychiatry*, August 1967, pp. 64-67. A report on one of only two experiments conducted on the effectiveness of A.A. which featured a control group and random assignment of subjects. Not as sophisticated as the Brandsma study, but important nonetheless.

"Alcoholism as a Self-Limiting Disease," by Leslie R.H. Drew. *Quarterly Journal of Studies on Alcohol,* No. 29, 1968, pp. 956-967. An important evalutation of many studies on rates of "spontaneous" recovery from alcoholism.

"Divine Intervention and the Treatment of Chemical Dependency," by Drs. Albert Ellis and Eugene Schoenfeld. *Journal of Substance Abuse,* No. 2, 1990, pp. 459-468 and 489-494. An enlightening analysis of the 12 Steps.

Heavy Drinking: They Myth of Alcoholism as a Disease, by Herb Fingarette. Berkeley, CA: University of California Press, 1988. A short but thorough discussion of the title topic.

"Does A.A. Really Work?," by Frederick B. Glaser and Alan C. Ogborne. *British Journal of Addiction*, 77 (1982), pp. 123-129. Discusses difficulty of accurately gauging A.A.'s effectiveness and suggests guidelines for conducting valid studies of A.A.

"The Extent of Long-Term Moderate Drinking Among Alcoholics Discharged from Medical and Psychiatric Treatment Facilities," John E. Helzer et al, eds. *The New England Journal of Medicine*, June 27, 1985, pp. 1678-1682. A report on a study of moderate drinking among a large population of bad-prognosis alcoholics.

Handbook of Alcoholism Treatment Approaches, Reid K. Hester & William R. Miller, eds. New York: Pergamon Press, 1989. Evaluations of various treatments for alcoholism. The section on A.A. is concise but packed with information.

The Diagnosis and Treatment of Alcoholism (2nd Ed.), by Jack H. Mendelson and Nancy K. Mello. New York: McGraw Hill, 1985. A standard alcoholism treatment text.

Treating Addictive Behaviors, William R. Miller & Nick Heather, eds. New York: Plenum Press, 1986. Contains an extremely valuable chapter on "The Effectiveness of Alcoholism Treatment: What Research Reveals," pp. 121-174. Probably the best currently available comparative evaluation.

"Evaluating Alcoholics Anonymous," by Alan C. Ogborne & Frederick B. Glaser. Chapter 6, pp. 176-192 in *Alcoholism and Substance Abuse: Strategies for Clinical Intervention*, Thomas E. Bratter & Gary G. Forrest, eds. New York: The Free Press, 1985. An indispensable study of the effectiveness of A.A. and the characteristics of those who affiliate with it (which presumably correlate with the characteristics of those alcoholics for whom A.A. is an appropriate treatment).

Diseasing of America, by Stanton Peele. Lexington, MA: Lexington Books, 1989. A well-written, well-documented attack on the concept of behavior as a disease.

"Recovery Without Treatment," by Thomas Prugh. *Alcohol Health and Research World*, Fall 1986, pp. 24 & 71-72. Brief review of studies of spontaneous remission of alcoholism.

"The Great Controlled-Drinking Controversy," by Ron Roizen, in *Recent Developments in Alcoholism, Vol. 5*, pp. 245-279. Good overview of this decades-long controversy.

"Alcoholics Anonymous and the Treatment and Prevention of Alcoholism," by Norman E. Zinberg. *Alcoholism: Clinical and Experimental Research*, January 1977, pp. 91-102. Useful discussion of the psychological aspects of A.A. as well as A.A.'s ideology.

"Spontaneous Remission in Alcoholics: Empirical Observations and Theoretical Implications," by Barry S. Tuchfeld. *Journal of Studies on Alcohol*, Vol. 42, No. 7, 1981, pp. 626-641. Contains very interesting excerpts from interviews with former alcoholics who overcame their drinking problems independently of any treatment program.

"Comments on A.A.'s Triennial Surveys." New York: Alcoholics Anonymous World Services, 1990. A very useful monograph on growth of and trends in A.A.'s membership.

CULTS

I Was a Mormon, by Einar Anderson. Grand Rapids, MI: Zondervan Publishing House, 1964. Informative attack on the Church of Jesus Christ of Latter Day Saints by a former Mormon turned fundamentalist Christian.

Inside the League, by Jon Lee Anderson and Scott Anderson. New York: Dodd Mead, 1986. Fascinating study of fascist and death squad influence within the World Anti-Communist League. Contains information on the political activities of the Moon organization.

Cults in America: Programmed for Paradise, by Willa Appel. New York: Henry Holt & Co., 1983. Not a description of particular cults, but a sociological and psychological analysis of the cult phenomenon.

Prophet of Blood: The Story of the "Mormon Manson", by Ben Bradlee, Jr. and Dale Van Atta. New York: Putnam Pub. Group, 1981. Incredible and gruesome account of Mormon polygamist cult leader Ervil LeBaron and his Church of the Blood of the Lambs of God.

The Irrational in Politics, by Maurice Brinton. San Francisco: Acrata Press, 1987. An updating of Wilhelm Reich's theories, focusing on why so many people are attracted to authoritarian political cults such as Nazism and Communism.

No Man Knows My History, by Fawn Brodie. New York: Knopf, 1946, 1971. Acclaimed historian Brodie's biography of Mormon founder Joseph Smith. Beautifully written, extremely well documented, and devastating.

L. Ron Hubbard: Messiah or Madman?, by Bent Corydon and L. Ron Hubbard, Jr. Secaucus, NJ: Lyle Stuart, 1987. A fascinating expose of L. Ron Hubbard, Sr. and his Church of Scientology by the ultimate insider, his son, with the aid of another former insider. Much of the material in this book is outright shocking. Unfortunately, *Messiah or Madman* is very poorly written and very poorly organized. This could have been a great book; but it isn't.

Crazy for God: The Nightmare of Cult Life, by Christopher Edwards. Englewood Cliffs, NJ: Prentice-Hall, 1979. A horrifying and informative account of life inside Sun Myung Moon's Unification Church.

Paradise Incorporated: Synanon, by David U. Gerstel. Novato, CA: Presidio Press, 1982. An account by an insider of Synanon during the years it was going haywire. Absolutely gripping. Overall, perhaps the best book written on any contemporary cult.

Brotherhood of Murder, by Thomas Martinez & John Guinther. New York: McGraw-Hill, 1988. A chilling insider's look at the most vicious political cult in recent years, The Order (Christian fundamentalist racists and terrorists).

Combatting Cult Mind Control, by Steven Hassan. Rochester, VT: Park Street Press, 1988. Excellent book on the psychological aspects of cults.

Lyndon LaRouche and the New American Fascism, by Dennis King. New York: Doubleday, 1989. The best source of information on the LaRouche cult.

Don't Call Me Brother: A Ringmaster's Escape from the Pentecostal Church, by Austin Miles. Buffalo, NY: Prometheus Books, 1989. An amazing account of the sleazy and cult-like aspects of evangelical Christianity by a prominent former Pentecostal minister.

Bare-Faced Messiah: The True Story of L. Ron Hubbard, by Russell Miller. New York: Henry Holt & Co., 1987. A thorough and competently written, if somewhat dry, biography of Church of Scientology founder and guru L. Ron Hubbard.

Six Years With God: Life Inside Rev. Jim Jones's Peoples Temple, by Jeannie Mills. New York: A&W Publishers, 1979. A poorly organized but riveting account of life inside Jim Jones' cult.

The Light on Synanon, by Dave Mitchell, Cathy Mitchell, and Richard Ofshe. New York: Seaview Books, 1980. An account of Synanon's berserk behavior by the journalists who exposed the cult's misdeeds. Well written and informative.

Apocalypse Delayed: The Story of Jehovah's Witnesses, by James Penton. Toronto: Toronto University Press, 1986. Probably the best single source of information on the Witnesses. Academic but thorough.

The Mass Psychology of Fascism, by Wilhelm Reich. New York: Farrar, Straus & Giroux, 1970. An extremely insightful analysis of the worst of the political cults, Nazism, and its mass appeal.

Prison or Paradise: The New Religious Cults, by James and Marcia Rudin. Philadelphia: Fortress Press, 1980. Contains brief but informative descriptions of the major religious cults, including Christian fundamentalist cults.

The Family, by Ed Sanders. New York: E.P. Dutton & Co., 1971. Probably the best, definitely the most entertaining, account of Charles Manson's "family."

30 Years a Watchtower Slave, by William J. Schnell. Grand Rapids, MI: Baker Book House, 1971. An expose of the Jehovah's Witnesses by a long-time member.

All Gods [sic] *Children: The Cult Experience — Salvation or Slavery,* by Carroll Stoner and Jo Anne Parke. New York: Penguin, 1977. A good description and analysis of American cults in the late 1970s.

Hostage to Heaven, by Barbara & Betty Underwood. New york: Clarkson N. Potter, Inc., 1979. While not as well written or gripping as *Crazy for God,* this is still a revealing and frightening insider's account of life in the Unification Church.

Index

A.A. (see Alcoholics Anonymous)
A.A. Service Manual, The 120
A.A. Way of Life, The. 51
A.A. The Way It Began. 31f, 53f
ABC of Anarchism 81f
About Anarchism. 81f
Adler, Alfred. 134
Adult Children of Alcoholics 5
Agnosticism (see Atheism)
Akron, Ohio. 37-40, 42, 43, 45, 47, 48, 92
Al-Anon 5, 49
Alateen 50
Alcoholic (definition) 103, 104, 116
Alcoholic Foundation. 41, 46
Alcoholics (population). 103-105
Alcoholics Anonymous 5-7, 9, 10, 13-15,
    23, 34-82, 92-126, 129
    General Service Board 41, 50, 51, 113f
    General Service Conference. 48, 49,
        51, 102
    General Service Office 11, 47, 50,
        51, 76, 77
    Group Service Representatives 49
    International Conventions 49, 51
    Latin America 117, 118
    Literature Sales 76
    Meeting Types 13, 15, 52
    Membership Characteristics 95,
        104-107, 112, 113, 114f, 116, 125
    Membership Totals 42, 47, 50, 52,
        53f, 106
    Organizational Structure 57, 58,
        73-75, 77-79, 84, 94
    Overseas 50, 117, 118
    Success Rate 106-111
Alcoholics Anonymous (book) 6, 16, 35,
    36, 39-44, 46, 49, 68, 93, 95, 103
Alcoholics Anonymous Comes of Age 16, 36,
    49, 55, 62
Alcoholism (definition) 103, 104
Alcoholism Treatment (A.A. influence/in-
    volvement) 9, 43, 52, 62, 76, 78,
    96-98, 107, 116, 117, 120
Alexander, Jack 45

Allentown *Morning Call.* 22
Allentown, Pennsylvania 17
AMA 38
Amalric, Arnold 90
American Atheists Addiction Recovery Groups
    (AAARG) 96, 97
American Humanist Association 126
American Psychological Association 141
American Radio Relay League 78
Amos, Frank 42
Anarchism and Anarcho-Syndicalism 81f
Anarchism (organizational theory and
    practices 58, 73-75, 77-79, 81f, 94, 102
Anarchy in Action 81f
Anonymity 48, 60, 61, 80, 81, 99, 102f
Anti-intellectualism 20, 58, 59, 83, 93,
    105, 119
Apartheid System. 22, 23
Aphorisms & Slogans. 59, 83, 93
As Bill Sees It 51
Atheism 15, 57, 66, 67, 134
Avakian, Bob 89
Aversion Therapies 112
Bakeland, Frederick. 105
Barefaced Messiah. 91f
Bartley, W.W. 137
Bean, Dr. Margaret 98
Belladonna Cure. 36
Belk, J. Blanton 30
Berkman, Alexander. 81f
Beziers Massacre 90
Bible 17, 18, 38, 43, 95
"Big Book" (see *Alcoholics Anonymous*)
Bill W. 53f
Binges (see Relapses)
Birmingham, Bill 27
Brandsma (study). 110, 111
Brinton, Maurice 54f
Bryn Mawr College 19
BSU Arbiter 88
Buchman, Frank. 16-33, 41, 44, 45, 51,
    55-60, 68, 70, 115, 118

Buchmanism (see Oxford Group Movement)
Bufe, Charles 5, 7
Buffalo, NY. 126
Burbank, Luther 119
Byrd, Admiral Richard 21
C., Bill (no. 1). 38
C., Bill (no. 2). 106
Cambridge University 19
Carnegie, Dale 44
Case Against Religiosity 62, 126, 127
Catholic Church. 39, 41, 138
Caux, Switzerland 27
Central Ideas of Alcoholism 129-131
Chamberlain, Neville. 126
Chiang Kai-Shek 29
Children of God 83
Christian Century, The. 25, 30
Christopher, Jim. 11, 124-126
Church of Jesus Christ of Latter Day Saints
   (see Mormons)
Church of Scientology 10, 82, 83, 86,
   89, 91f, 98
Church of the Blood of the Lambs of God . . .
   83, 84, 89
Church Times, The 22
Cleveland, Ohio 43
Cleveland Plain Dealer 45
Client Matching. 112, 113
Coca-Cola Corporation 30-31
CODESH (Council for Democratic and
   Secular Humanism 124, 126
Collectives in the Spanish Revolution. 81f
Collegiate Association for the Research of
   Principles 88
Communists. 23, 25, 28, 29
Community Reinforcement Approach . . . . . .
   111, 112
Confederación Nacional del Trabajo 78
Confession of Sins 19, 36, 55, 56, 68, 69, 115
Confrontation. 112
Continuance. 55, 68, 71, 72
Controlled Drinking. 111, 112
Cooper, Paulette. 89
Corydon, Bent. 91f
Courage to Change, The 103
Crowning Experience, The 22
Daley, Dennis. 65, 66
Decentralism. 75
Dederich, Charles 84, 102
Denial 65, 66, 68
Disease Concept of Alcoholism 5, 62,
   67, 68, 108
Disulfiram (Antabuse) 112

Ditman et al (study) 109, 110
Divine Guidance 19, 20, 23-26, 28,
Divine Guidance 19, 20, 23-26, 28, 32f,
   38, 39, 44, 55-59, 66, 67, 71, 115, 117, 118
"Divine Intervention and the Treatment of
   Chemical Dependency" 6, 62
Doctor Bob (see Smith, Dr. Robert)
Dr. Bob and the Good Old Timers 53f
Dodge, Mr. & Mrs. Cleveland 21
Draft Evasion (MRA) 26
Dreikurs, Rudolf 134
Driberg, Tom. 27
Eddy, Sherwood 17
Edison, Mrs. Thomas 21
Einstein, Albert 57
Ellis, Dr. Albert 5-7, 11, 62-64, 67, 126, 127
Emerson, Ralph Waldo 123
Employee Assistance Quarterly. 6
Escape from Utopia. 91f
Evangelical Lutheran Ministerium of
   Pennsylvania. 17
Fascism. 23, 24, 32f, 54f
Fascism and Big Business 54f
FBI 85
Feigl, Herbert. 137
Fields, Factories and Workshops Tomorrow 81f
Firestone, Russell. 21
Five "Cs". 68, 69, 71, 72
For a Change 30
Ford, Mr. & Mrs. Henry. 21
Fosdick, Dr. Harry Emerson. 44, 46, 93
Four Absolutes 20
Free Inquiry. 124, 126
Freud, Dr. Sigmund. 35, 134
Fromm, Erich. 134
Gamblers Anonymous 118
General Electric 30
Getting Better 15f, 53f
Glaser, Frederick. 114f
Grandberg V. Ashland County. 92
Grapevine, The 47, 48, 73
Group Therapy 105, 112
Growth Through Reason. 142
Guerin, Daniel 54f
Guggenheim, Mrs. Harry 21
Guidance (see Divine Guidance)
H., Roland 35, 41, 50
Hadley, William S. 41
Handbook of Rational-Emotive Therapy 142
Hare Krishnas 82, 83, 86, 87
Harper & Brothers 42
Harper, Robert. 136

Hartford Seminary 17-19
Harvard University 19
Heather, Nick 112
Heatter, Gabriel 44
Herman, Ellen 56
Hibden, John 19, 31f
Higher Power 6, 7, 14, 48, 64, 66, 67,
    69, 82, 93
Himmler, Heinrich 25
Hitler, Adolf 9, 10, 23, 24, 26, 32f,
    39, 45, 135, 138
Hofmeyr, J.H. 22
Homage to Catalonia 81f
Homophobia 28, 29, 32f, 33f, 58
Horney, Karen 134, 142
Hospitalization 43
Houseparties 18, 21, 55
How to Stay Sober 125
Howard, Peter 29, 30
Hubbard, L. Ron Jr. 91f
Humanist, The 129
Humanist Party 85
Humanistic Psychotherapy: The Rational-Emotive
    Approach 142
Ideology and Co-Existence 28, 29
Incest Survivors Anonymous 118
Institute for Rational Emotive Therapy . . . 145
International Socialists 85
International Society for Krishna
    Consciousness (see Hare Krishnas)
Irrational in Politics, The 54
IWW 78
Jaffe, Aniela 54f
Jahoda, Marie 134
James, Williams 36, 41
Jehovah's Witnesses 83, 89
Jones, Rev. Jim 87
Jonestown 87
Journal of Rational Recovery 126
Journal of Substance Abuse 6
Journal of the American Medical Association 44
Jung: A Biography 54f
Jung's Last Years 54f
Jung, Dr. Carl 35, 41, 50, 51, 54f, 134
Kennedy, Dr. Foster 46
Keswick, England 17, 70
Key Men 20, 32f, 60
Kirkpatrick, Jean 123, 134, 128
Kropotkin, Peter 81f
Ku Klux Klan 139
Kuling, China 18
Kurtz, Ernest 53f

L. Ron Hubbard: Messiah or Madman? 91f
Labor (MRA influence) 27, 28
Larouche, Lyndon 86
LaRouche Cult 82, 83, 85, 86, 88
Lean, Garth 32f
LeBaron, Ervil 83, 90f
Lee, John Doyle 90
Leval, Gaston 81f
Liberty 44
Life Changers (see Soul Surgeons)
Light On Synanon, The 102f
Lindsay, Kenneth 25
Little Rock, Arkansas 45
London, William 114f
Lord's Prayer 15, 93
LSD 50, 53f
Mackinac Island, Michigan 27
Mahoney, Michael 137
Mann, Marty 47, 75
Markey, Morris 44
Marx, Karl 23
Maslow, Abraham 134
Mass Psychology of Fascism, The 54f
May, Rollo 134
McCarthy, Senator Joe 29
Men for Sobriety 63, 124
Mensa 78
Miami, Florida 51
Milennarianism 89, 101
Miller, Russell 91f
Miller, William 112
Mills, Jeannie 91f
Moonies (see Unification Church)
Moral Re-Armament (see Oxford Group
    Movement)
Moral Rearmament Campaign 25, 26
Morantz, Paul 89
Mormons 82, 83, 86, 87, 90
Mount Airy Seminary 17
Mountain Meadows Massacre 90, 91f
Muhlenberg College 16
Munich Conference 26
Mystery of Moral Re-Armament, The 27
Mussolini, Benito 23
Narcotics Anonymous 52, 118
National Committee for Education on
    Alcoholism (see NCA)
National Council on Alcohol (see NCA)
National Council on Alcoholism and Other
    Drug Addictions (see NCA)
National Organization for Women 78
National Rubber Machinery Co. 37, 38

Nazism (see Fascism)

NCA 47, 75, 103

NCEA (see NCA)

New Ageism 70

New Alliance Party 83, 85, 87

New York City 34-42, 44-47, 49, 50

New York Herald Tribune 45, 93

New York Times 29, 44

New York World Telegram 23-25, 32f

Newman, John Henry 21

Niacin 51

Niebuhr, Reinhold 45

1984 93

Non-A.A. 12-Step Organizations 49,
   50, 52, 53, 118-120

Not God 53f

Ogborne, Alan. 114f

Ohl, Dr. J.F. 17

Olin, William 91f

On the Tail of a Comet 32f

Orwell, George 81f

Overbrook, Pennsylvania 17

Overeaters Anonymous 6, 118

Oxford Group Movement 9, 10, 16-33,
   35-44, 55-62, 65-72, 92, 93, 115

Oxford Groups (see Oxford Group Movement)

Oxford Movement 21

Oxford University 19, 21

P., Hank 42

Paradise Incorporated: Synanon 102f

Pass It On 23, 24, 35, 53f

Peale, Norman Vincent 123

Peele, Stanton 121f

People's Temple . . . 10, 82, 84-87, 91f, 98, 100

Perls, Fritz 134

Philadelphia, Pennsylvania 17

Pigeons 55

Pittman, Bill. 31f, 53f

Popper, Karl 137

Powerlessness. 55, 65, 66, 69, 74, 115, 118

Princeton University. 19, 31f

Prison or Paradise. 83

Prognosticative Factors (alcoholism
   treatment). 105, 109

Progressive Labor Party 85

Quarterly Journal of Studies on Alcohol. 106

Quiet Time. 17, 19, 38, 57

R., Morgan. 44

Racism 58

Rational Behavior Therapy. 110, 111

Rational Emotive Therapy 5-7, 111,
   126, 127, 134, 137-139, 141-145

*Rational-Emotive Therapy and Cognitive
   Behavior Therapy* 142

*Ration-Emotive Treatment of Alcoholic and Drug
   Abusers* 6

Rational Recovery 6, 7, 63, 97, 101,
   126, 127, 129-131

*Rational Recovery from Alcoholism: The Small
   Book* 126

Reader's Digest. 42, 44

Reader's Digest Foundation 30

Reader's Guide to Periodical Literature 26, 27

Reason and Growth in Psychotherapy 142

Red Cross 78

Reich, Wilhelm 53f

Reichenbach, Hans 137

Relapse (alcoholic). 65, 66, 111

Religiomania 36, 41

Research Institute on Alcoholism 114f

Restitution 20, 36, 55, 71, 115

RET (see Rational Emotive Therapy)

Revolutionary Communist Party 83, 89

Revolving Door Effect 106, 107

Richardson, Willard 41, 46

Riffe, John 28

Robens, Lord 27

Robertson, Nan 15f, 53f

Rockefeller, John D. Jr. 41, 42, 45-47

Rockefeller, Nelson 46

Rocker, Rudolf 81f

Rogers, Carl. 134, 138

R.R. (see Rational Recovery)

Rudin, James 83

Rudin, Martha. 83

Russell, Bertrand 137

S., Clarence 43

St. Francis. 141

St. Theresa 141

Salvation Army. 17

San Francisco. 15, 97, 106

Saturday Evening Post 45

Schoenfeld, Dr. Eugene. 11, 62, 63, 67

Science of Mind 139

Scientology (see Church of Scientology)

Secular Organizations for Sobriety 7,
   63, 97, 101, 111, 114f, 124-126, 131

Seiberling, Henrietta 37

Serenity Prayer. 14, 45

Sexaholics Anonymous 118

Sexism. 58

Sharpeville Massacre 22

Shoemaker, Sam. 16

Silkworth, Dr. William 35, 40, 51, 68

Skinner, B.F. 129
Smith, Anne 37, 38, 48
Smith, Dr. Robert 16, 37-39, 41-43,
   45-48, 51, 56, 62, 75, 92, 94, 102
Sobriety Priority 125
Social Skills Training 112
Social Work 65
Socialist Workers Party 85
S.O.S. (see Secular Organizations for Sobriety)
Soul Surgeons 20, 55, 69
South Africa 21-23
Spiritual Awakening/Experiences 36,
   41, 72, 93
Spiritualism 48
Sponsors 56, 69
Spontaneous Recovery 108, 109
Stalin, Josef 135
Stearly, Garrett 32f
Stress Management 112
Strong, Leonard 35, 41
Suggested Guidelines for Sobriety 125,
   131, 132
Synanon 10, 82-84, 86, 87, 89, 100, 102
T., Ebby 35, 36, 41
13 Statements of Acceptance 124, 128
Thomsen, Robert 53f
Time 18, 27
Tobacco 13-15, 51
Towns, Charles B. 42
Towns Hospital 35, 36, 40
Traveling Teams 20, 22
Trillin, Calvin 30
Trimpey, Jack 6, 126
Tunks, Walter 37

12 Steps 5-7, 9, 10, 15, 16, 40, 41, 44,
   48, 49, 53, 55, 56, 62-73, 93-96, 100, 115,
   118-120, 128, 133
12 Steps & 12 Traditions 49, 55, 73, 74,
   77, 78, 97
12 Traditions 47, 48, 58, 73-81, 94, 102
Unification Church 83-88, 93, 100
Unhooked 125
Union Club Dinner 46, 47
Up with People! 30, 31
U.S. Chess Federation 78
Varieties of Religious Experience 36, 41
Volvo Corp. 31
Walter, Nicolas 81f
Ward, Colin 81f
Washingtonian Society 79, 97
Way International, The 83
Way Out, The 40
Wehr, Gerhard 54f
WFS (see Women for Sobriety)
Wholely, Dennis 103
Wilson, Bill 9, 16, 23, 34,-52, 55, 56,
   58, 61, 62, 67, 68, 73-75, 77-79, 92, 94, 97,
   102, 103, 118
Wilson, Gilman 34
Wilson (Burnham), Lois 34, 35, 37, 38,
   45, 46
Wittgenstein, Ludwig 137
Women for Sobriety 7, 63, 97,
   123-125, 128
Works Publishing Company 42
Yale University 19, 61
YMCA 17

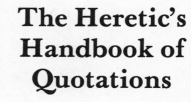